ROUTLEDGE LIBRARY EDITIONS:
THE LABOUR MOVEMENT

Volume 39

LABOUR RELATIONS AND POLITICAL CHANGE IN EASTERN EUROPE

LABOUR RELATIONS AND POLITICAL CHANGE IN EASTERN EUROPE

A Comparative Perspective

Edited by
JOHN THIRKELL, RICHARD SCASE
AND SARAH VICKERSTAFF

Routledge
Taylor & Francis Group

LONDON AND NEW YORK

First published in 1992 by Routledge

This edition first published in 2019
by Routledge
2 Park Square, Milton Park, Abingdon, Oxon OX14 4RN

and by Routledge
711 Third Avenue, New York, NY 10017

Routledge is an imprint of the Taylor & Francis Group, an informa business

British Library Cataloguing in Publication Data
A catalogue record for this book is available from the British Library

ISBN: 978-1-138-32435-0 (Set)
ISBN: 978-0-429-43443-3 (Set) (ebk)
ISBN: 978-1-138-32583-8 (Volume 38) (hbk)
ISBN: 978-1-138-32585-2 (Volume 38) (pbk)
ISBN: 978-0-429-45021-1 (Volume 38) (ebk)

Publisher's Note
The publisher has gone to great lengths to ensure the quality of this reprint but points out that some imperfections in the original copies may be apparent.

Disclaimer
The publisher has made every effort to trace copyright holders and would welcome correspondence from those they have been unable to trace.

Labour relations and political change in eastern Europe

A comparative perspective

Edited by

John Thirkell, Richard Scase
and Sarah Vickerstaff

UCL
PRESS

First published in 1995 by UCL Press

UCL Press Limited
University College London
Gower Street
London WC1E 6BT

The name of University College London (UCL) is a registered
trade mark used by UCL Press with the consent of the owner.

British Library Cataloguing-in-Publication Data
A CIP catalogue record for this book is available from the British Library.

ISBN: 1-85728-348-1 HB

Typeset in Times Roman.
Printed and bound by
Biddles Ltd, Guildford and King's Lynn, England.

Contents

v

Introduction

John Thirkell, Richard Scase, Sarah Vickerstaff

It is the contention of this book that labour relations are a key constituent element in the transformation of eastern European and Russian society. At the national level, governments' strategies of "shock therapy" or "gradualism" are tempered by the threat or potential for industrial unrest, and the trade unions have often played a critical role in mobilizing consent for economic reform. At enterprise level, attempts to transform the property structure and the relations of production are constrained and conditioned by the traditional approaches of management and workers developed over the long period of the command economy. The strength and persistence of these enterprise based patterns and habits varies from country to country, according to recent past policies of economic reform and the specific processes of regime collapse in each case. Nevertheless, in all cases labour relations at enterprise level remain of critical significance in the success or failure of different change strategies. The need to restructure the labour process and to introduce capitalist patterns of labour control are the necessary corollary of the attempt to transform the economy into a largely privately-owned market system. The difficulty of doing this in practice is what makes labour relations a key issue for regime change.

Thus we have sought to focus upon changes in patterns of labour relations associated with privatization and organizational restructuring in the selected countries of Bulgaria, the Czech and Slovak republics, Hungary, Poland and the Siberian region of Russia. The dramatic changes that are occurring in these countries are becoming more central to academic debate. However, there are two features of the existing body of

1

literature which are problematic. First, most discussions tend to be excessively theoretical and often empirically unfounded. Secondly, when research has been undertaken it has tended to focus upon particular trends *within* specific countries. The purpose of this book is to focus upon trends as they are occurring *between* countries drawing upon detailed *empirical* research studies.

This book arises out of a collaborative research project, over the three years up to 1994, which has investigated enterprise level changes in labour relations in eastern Europe. The research design and methodology was agreed by the international research team at the beginning of the project. The empirical research is based upon in-depth enterprise case studies in each of the countries and has been guided and developed throughout by the frequent meetings of the team. The fieldwork was undertaken by local researchers in each country, regular reports on the progress of case studies were given to the international team, and members of the British group made regular visits to the individual eastern European countries. At the outset of the research it was agreed that local fieldworkers would provide the best means of covering a broad range of enterprises across six countries. Each of the chapters in this book is interrelated by shared theoretical, methodological and empirical perspectives derived from the collaboration of the contributors.

The project was funded by a grant from the Economic and Social Research Council (ESRC) under its East–West Initiative and has provided a unique opportunity for comparative research into labour relations changes in eastern Europe. In connection with the eastern European research initiative, the ESRC has run a series of workshops in which recipients of grants have benefited from contact with each other and from early access to research results.

At the beginning of the research project it was agreed that at this point in the transformation of eastern European societies it is not possible, or fruitful, to use western European models of labour relations as benchmarks against which the developing systems can be evaluated. Although such attempts provide some useful insights (see, for example, Slomp 1992; Moerel 1994) they tend systematically to underplay the differences between the countries of eastern Europe and the "path dependent" character of their transformation. As we discuss below, we do not see these societies as being simply in transition to an already existing model of a market economy. Indeed, the trajectories of their transformation leaves uncertain the relevance of industrial relations models drawn from other parts of Europe.

It was decided to focus the research, therefore, upon a number of key issues associated with the period of transformation. These themes provided both the hypotheses for the research and the basis for structuring the case study enquiries. These are as follows: in the command economy, enterprises had very little room for independent action. It is, therefore, to be expected that the privatization and restructuring of the economies will lead to greater autonomy of enterprises in which emerging processes of corporate strategy formulation will be critical. Our first research theme was to consider the development of enterprise strategies, how they are shaped, both by broader external and internal organizational forces and by the extent to which these are leading to a redefinition of labour relations issues. Within this context, the role of middle management is vital, since, as part of the strategy implementation process, its plays a key role in emergent forms of labour relations within enterprises. The second research question is to explore the manner in which organizational restructuring is changing the role of middle management in labour relations.

Our third area of interest is the impact of privatization and restructuring on the role of trade unions at both national and corporate levels. The strategies of trade unions towards ownership change and its consequences will provide a major source of support or constraint on transformation processes. Fourthly, we would expect forms of collective bargaining to develop as trade unions are transformed from transmission belts into more independent forces in political and economic management. In view of the eastern European state tradition, legislative changes at a national level are likely to have a variable impact within enterprises, depending upon the constellation of bargaining forces, the market position of enterprises, and many other factors. With privatization and the restructuring of organizations, other forms of interest articulation are appearing as traditional patterns of organizational control disappear. This applies both to managers and to shopfloor employees. The fifth theme the research explores is emerging sources of interest differentiation and how these are being articulated through various institutional and non-institutional mechanisms. We also consider the survival of earlier forms of "self-management".

In addition to these largely enterprise-based issues, the research focuses upon two broader themes which we believed will be critical in defining or constraining the enterprise arena. Changes within enterprises are being driven by a range of external processes within which political parties, national government processes and labour unions play key roles. The research also explores the extent to which new forms of tripartism and corporatism develop to condition enterprise level labour relations. Finally, many of the changes, as these are affecting labour relations, have as their "model" the practice of some Western countries. Such models are often promoted by international agencies such as the World Bank or the International Monetary Fund (IMF) as part of macro-economic stabilization measures. Certain models may also be encouraged by the International Labour Office (ILO) and international trade unions. At enterprise level, Western consultants, joint ventures or foreign take-overs may result in the transference of Western ideas and practices in labour relations. These processes of transference are another area of our research enquiry, although they do not figure largely in this book.

Given the nature of these research themes it was agreed that a case study methodology, as opposed to large-scale survey techniques, would provide the best means by which to track changes in enterprise-level labour relations. Although surveys may have provided broader quantitative data they could not have provided the opportunity to look at the processes of change. Hence, using case studies it is possible to explore the interplay between external and internal organizational forces as these affect patterns of labour relations. Continuities and discontinuities can be investigated and, particularly, the extent and likelihood of emerging patterns becoming institutionalized. The period over which the research was undertaken enables a qualitative assessment of the process of organizational change.

In deciding upon the choice of case studies, a number of factors were significant. It was first considered whether to try and match the sample of enterprises in terms of their stage in the privatization process. This was rejected because the progress of ownership change was extremely variable from country to country and the governmental programmes for privatization were still in a considerable state of flux. Within each country it was decided to try and find a range of enterprises which represented the traditional areas of "socialist industry", namely state enterprises in manufacturing, especially engineering. Although very interesting, the emerging private small service sector was rejected as a focus because of the traditional weakness and underdeveloped nature of the service sector in the communist eras. The real task of transformation in these economies will be to change the industrial structure, and within this the viability of existing large enterprises is a critical issue. For both economic and ideological reasons the survival of such enterprises raises fundamental issues in the sphere of labour relations. The ease with which large organizations can be privatized and the broader employment implications of this suggest that these enterprises are likely to play a key role in public perceptions of economic policy. The traditional view of the enterprise as community and the emphasis on industrial workers as the vanguard of socialism also suggests that the task of transforming labour relations in prominent industries will be critical. We therefore sought case study enterprises which were illustrative of these themes. We do not claim that the cases are representative of all sectors, but rather that they are indicative of key change processes. The choice also includes some critical or prototype cases. Basic information about the case study enterprises is provided in Table 1.

The case study research proceeded by regular visits to the chosen plants. In the initial phases researchers identified key informants at each level; senior, middle and junior management, trade union leaders, other

Table 1 Case study enterprises.

BULGARIA	BOS AIR Air transport	FLEX TOOL Hand tools, motors	STARTCOM Electric motors	FERROMOULD Foundry
CZECH/ SLOVAK	SPRINGS Mechanical springs	SLOVCAR Car manufacturer	FLOORPLAST Plastic products	
HUNGARY	HUNGAIR Air transport	PROMED Medical equipment	FERROCOR Steel	
POLAND	COLDCUTS Food	MEDEX Medical equipment	POLTOOLS Industrial tools	POWCOM Electro-techniques
RUSSIA (Primary cases)	ELMACH Metal rolling	LEBAGS Leather haberdashery	SIBERTURB Large electrical machines	MATOOLS Machine tools
RUSSIA (Secondary cases)	AERO Air transport	ALMETAL Aluminium ingots	FOUNDRY Foundry equipment	

worker representatives, and shopfloor workers. These contacts were maintained over subsequent visits and new informants were used where appropriate. It was also necessary to develop a brief historical picture of recent past developments in the enterprise as the backdrop to recent developments. Documentary sources and interviews furnished this material and in some cases researchers had previous experience of the enterprise. During return visits field workers were also able to observe production processes and attend workers' meetings or management sessions. Researchers also had the opportunity to follow up issues which the international research group as a whole identified as being important or of comparative significance.

In addition to developing the case study material the national teams of researchers also collected information about the broader economic and political context of labour relations changes. This included documentary sources of various kinds (for example, laws, collective agreements, contracts) and in some cases interviews with trade union officials, employers and commentators outside the enterprises. Throughout the research project the team collectively and individually took every opportunity to present papers to conferences and have benefited greatly from the critical comments and queries of other researchers engaged in similar and related fields.

Chapter 1 provides a comparative overview of changes in labour relations in the different countries and is focused mainly at the national level. Subsequent chapters consider the developments at enterprise level by reference to a detailed analysis of the case study organizations in each of the selected countries. Changes at this level are also situated in the context of wider national political and economic issues. The final chapter concludes by reviewing the key processes of change in labour relations at enterprise level focusing upon emergent tendencies and the degrees of similarity and difference between the countries.

CHAPTER 1

Changing models of labour relations in eastern Europe and Russia

John Thirkell, Richard Scase, Sarah Vickerstaff

This introduction provides a comparative framework for the discussion of transitions in labour relations in a number of selected countries in the former eastern Europe; Bulgaria, the Czech and Slovak republics, Hungary, Poland and Russia. The following chapters take as their subject the changes within each of these countries. Under the former political regimes, the common features of state ownership of enterprises, party political control and central planning shaped the general character of labour relations models, but with the transition to market economies and political pluralism there are a number of concomitant changes in labour relations which are occurring at both the national and enterprise levels. We begin with an overview of the theoretical and empirical issues associated with the comparative study of labour relations in contemporary eastern Europe. We then proceed to consider the key themes that constitute the bases for analyzing changes in labour relations in the different chapters. The discussion also attempts to identify emerging similarities and differences in trends within the different countries. It argues that in the transition to various forms of market economy, labour relations models in each of the countries will be characterized by contrasting features, linked as they are to prevailing economic and political conditions.

Transition or transformation?

The contemporary literature on eastern Europe tends to be concerned with the nature of the "transition" that each country is facing. The complexity of the task of attempting to create democratic political institutions while transforming the nature of property relations dramatically is without precedent in recent world history. It is hardly surprising, in this "test bed" or "laboratory" for theorists of political democracy and societal transformation, that changes in labour relations have been somewhat neglected. Most contemporary discussions focus upon either political changes or macroeconomic developments, with labour relations receiving considerably less attention. The development of new patterns of labour relations is highly dependent upon the prevailing economic conditions, which in turn are conditioned by political processes. This "contingent" nature of labour relations changes would suggest that it is too early to determine the character of labour relations at the enterprise level, because new patterns have yet to be consolidated. However, developments in labour relations are constituent elements in a jigsaw of transformation processes because, in the past, the economic enterprise was the institutional articulation of political control. Hence, attempts to transform the polity are constrained by an "underdeveloped" civil society. Equally, attempts to transform the relations of production are hampered by the habits of management and workers which have evolved over a long period under the conditions of the former command economy.

The concept of *transition* has been challenged by some commentators as value-laden and deterministic, implying that each of these societies is "on the road" to capitalism. Stark (1992) has argued that the concept of *transformation* is preferable because it highlights *differences* between the eastern European countries and does not prejudge the likely outcomes. In the field of labour relations we would argue that this notion is valid in the sense of transition *from* a particular model of "Soviet" labour relations. However, the issue of transition *to* remains an open question. The concept of transformation is useful for describing the dynamic processes unfolding in each country but it needs to be operationalized in order to be useful both analytically and theoretically. We take it to refer to issues of continuity and discontinuity, and to similarities and differences between countries and, as such, it refers generally to broad issues of societal change.

8

Comparative labour relations has tended to be concerned with the extent to which models converge, or not, depending upon the level of development of the economy of which they are a part. The collapse of the Soviet-derived models of labour relations raises questions of the extent to which marketization and privatization of the eastern European economies will, in the longer term, result in a convergence with models of the western European pattern. Of course, convergence can be engineered to a certain extent by policy transference, that is, as a result of the behest of international agencies such as the (IMF) or the World Bank, or it may result from the implementation of management techniques associated with company take-overs and joint ventures. However, although policy transference may be significant, it is largely conditioned and constrained by indigenous development within the various countries of eastern Europe.

The context of change

The general elements of the model of labour relations under the previous political regimes are well known. They tended to conform to an economic model of central planning, party political control and state ownership. Trade unions operated within these parameters with job grades and associated pay rates fixed nationally by "tariff scales". Although there were collective agreements, there was no recognition of the right to collective bargaining or to strike. Trade union structure conformed to that of the branch (industry) ministries and operated on the principles of "democratic centralism". However, institutions for employee participation in management, and in some countries "self management", were highly developed, either through the structures of enterprise councils or at lower organizational levels such as with the brigades in Bulgaria and Czechoslovakia. Indeed, despite cross-national similarities in the centralization of political control, there were significant variations in the nature of enterprise-level employee participation, and these differences may well be reflected in contemporary developments. Stark (1992), for example, makes a parallel point with regard to processes of privatization; he argues that the key factors which condition the *direction* of transformation are patterns of political mobilization prior to regime collapse and the particular paths of extrication from the stranglehold of the Communist Party.

9

Consideration of the emerging models of labour relations in eastern Europe has to recognize that these have been contingent upon three factors. First, that political attention to processes of transition has centred on issues of democracy and marketization, that is, on the parallel processes of change in the political institutions and of changes in the management of the economy. Secondly, that the economic and social context has been one of inflation, rising unemployment and reductions in living standards for many sectors of the population. For post-communist governments, the central political issue has been to set up structures and mechanisms for the creation of market economies while at the same time maintaining a minimum level of social and political integration. Specifically this has meant them choosing the pace and sequence of macroeconomic measures – either the shock treatment of rapid change (the liberal market) or a more gradual approach (the social market). In such economic conditions trade unions often function as agencies of social integration through their informal relations and negotiations with governments. Attempts to establish political pluralism have meant the replacement of old Party organizations by a plethora of political parties which are often little more than "elite vehicles", in which popular membership is low by comparison with that of the communist parties they have replaced (Kolankiewcz 1993). Consequently, trade unions as organizations with *mass* memberships are in a position to fulfil a representational function for their rank-and-file members that is only partially undertaken by political parties. Thirdly, privatization has taken various forms – including intermediate forms of state ownership – and has progressed at different rates in the various countries. However, in each case the state remains – directly or indirectly – the main employer as well as the major agency for mechanisms of macroeconomic policy. Indeed, the privatization process requires state-driven social engineering on an unprecedented scale, which an ideology of "liberal" marketization tends to obscure. As Offe (1991) has commented, privatization in eastern Europe involves a process of "political capitalism" or "capitalism by design". Consequently, emerging models of labour relations are highly contingent upon patterns of political mobilization and upon a minimum level of political consensus. The institutionalization of new models of labour relations in these unstable conditions is, therefore, uncertain and in some countries complicated by governments' attempts to introduce normative frameworks in advance of economic reform and privatization. To investigate the transformation of labour relations we need to consider both changes at the national level (that is, the developing legislation and national framework and its impact on the enterprise level), and the relative autonomy of enterprises in responding to and initiating changes. We begin by looking at the process of ownership change as one factor of change in labour relations.

Marketization and ownership change

The constraints on enterprise autonomy within the planned economy meant that the scope for enterprise strategy was limited, that is, the choice of markets, the design of enterprise structures and the nature of labour relations. The market economy in theory enlarges the scope for enterprise strategy, although in the context of eastern Europe and Russia the concept of "marketization" is a complex one. In part, it involves processes of deregulation, price liberalization, and relating prices more closely to costs. In the centralized economy the most important source of state revenue was a turnover tax on enterprises and this can still be important as, for example, in Bulgaria. In general, processes of marketization can be seen as involving five main stages: (a) the exposure of state owned companies to market forces by the reduction (though not necessarily the abolition) of state subsidies and state orders, and with it a reduction in the allocative function of ministries; (b) deregulation of prices and wages and giving enterprises more autonomy in these areas; (c) competition in product markets and suppliers; (d) organizational restructuring, typically involving degrees of decentralization and divisionalization; and (e) changes in ownership. However, it is important to stress that these processes were under way in some countries before the collapse of the communist regimes and that, further, this sequence varies in different orders and at varying speeds between the different countries. There are often elements of continuity in some of these processes such that it is difficult to refer simply to "before" and "after" phases of regime collapse.

In the process of marketization, ownership change is only *one* aspect, despite the primary role it tends to be given in both Eastern and some Western approaches to economic reform. State ownership has normally been regarded as the fundamental basis of both the economy and of labour relations in state socialist countries. From this it is deduced that the prerequisite for changing the nature of enterprises and the behaviour of managers and employees is to change patterns of ownership on the assumption that changing the economy has to be based on transforming property relations. However, the relationship between ownership change, enterprise behaviour and labour relations is *in reality* more complex, and privatization is only one, and not always the most important, aspect of the process of marketization.

In considering the relationship between privatization and labour relations it is necessary to draw a distinction between the privatization of large industrial enterprises and that of small enterprises whether engaged in production, retail or other services. As Kozek (1993) and Cziria & Munkova (1991) show, in the latter there is often a sharp fall in union membership, with relations between management and workforce becoming "individualized". In larger state organizations there are three direct questions relating to labour relations. First, whether employees – or their representatives – are formally allocated a role in the process of ownership change. Secondly, whether employees – or their representatives – are accorded any proprietorial status following privatization. Thirdly, whether in such cases "formal" change has any substantive significance.

In relation to the first question, the national models fall into two groups. In Russia and Poland, endorsement from employees or their representatives is required for changes of ownership, whereas in Hungary, the Czech and Slovak republics and Bulgaria it is not. The consent of the labour collective is required in Russia while in Poland the agent is the Employee Council. At present, the predominant form of ownership change is to that of the joint stock company based on share ownership. In practice there are a variety of options which include both individual and institutional mechanisms in varying combinations. Individual shareholders may be employees, managers and citizens in general, while institutional forms include state agencies, other enterprises and banks. From the standpoint of labour relations the basic division is between those which include employee share ownership as a matter of legal right and those which do not. Again, Russia and Poland are in this category with the Polish model – unique in eastern Europe – having provision for union representation on supervisory boards. In Hungary and the Czech and Slovak republics there is, at present, no provision for employee shareholding as such, although in the Czech and Slovak republics employees may hold some shares acquired by them as citizens. However, in relation to the general issue of enterprise autonomy, a key issue is the nature of institutional share ownership and control. With the exception of the Czech republic there are, as yet, no share concentrations among financial institutions of the kind found in Britain and the United States.

Processes of marketization are complex, and a rapid and smooth transition to what is normally regarded as "the market economy" in the West is far from being achieved. Exposure to marketization, which in the first instance often means the reduction of state orders, is frequently associated with the internal restructuring of enterprises, usually initiated by enterprise management but sometimes in collaboration with state agencies. Such restructuring, whether directly or indirectly related to changes in ownership, is usually geared to breaking up the enterprise into different product areas. This process – often of divisionalization and decentralization – gives management the opportunity, usually for the first time, to develop business strategies. That is, to develop specific markets and products, and to implement appropriate organizational structures and mechanisms of enterprise change. Senior managers become engaged in a sequence of strategy and structural change, often in the direction of divisionalization, in order to secure more effective relations with product markets (Chandler 1962). Internal restructuring and divisionalization also have implications for labour relations since they can lead to the segmentation of internal labour markets.

The relationship between ownership change – as a stage in marketization – organizational restructuring, and changes in labour relations is often complex, for three reasons. First, processes of ownership change vary significantly both between and within countries. The principal forms *affecting large state enterprises* include: state leasing agreements; the creation of joint stock companies with the state as the only shareholder; foreign take-overs; joint ventures; and companies owned by large numbers of individual shareholders. Sometimes there are provisions for employee share ownership, for both managers and workers. In the longer term the balance of control between internal and external stakeholders is likely to have a significant influence on enterprise strategy. The third reason is that in eastern Europe, though much less so in Russia, new frameworks, institutions and mechanisms have been established at national level for the regulation of industrial relations (Thirkell et al. 1994). These include new and reconstructed trade union confederations, the legal recognition of strikes and of collective bargaining, and the development of national and occasionally local tripartite institutions. General Agreements negotiated at national level in Hungary, Bulgaria and the Czech and Slovak republics have been significant forces influencing the conduct of labour relations and therefore of managerial strategies at the enterprise level.

In practice, the pace of privatization varies considerably from country to country, and since it has generally been slower than was anticipated, the state remains a very significant employer. In addition, the state is likely to continue to be a major player in economic reform in the foreseeable future. However, as the following chapters suggest, even in the absence of ownership change, most enterprises have begun to restructure either in the face of changing markets for their products and/or in preparation for privatization. Offe (1991) has identified a "dilemma of simultaneity" in the political sphere where new nations, new constitutions and new party politics have to be created simultaneously. In the field of labour relations we can identify similar problems of trying to reconstruct labour codes and normative frameworks suitable for a market economy and pluralist democracy. This may result in what has been characterized as pre-emptive normative regulation (Offe 1991). We might therefore expect a continuing tension between the national and enterprise levels of labour relations. To some extent trade unions are a vehicle for this potential dissonance and it is to them we turn next.

The role of trade unionism

Generally, except in Russia, the first changes in existing models of labour relations occurred with the emergence of specific *alternatives* to already established trade union organizations. This was the case with Solidarity in Poland in 1982 and the emergence of new trade unions in Hungary in the autumn of 1988 affiliated to the Democratic League, facilitated by the law on associations and political pluralism. This was equally so in Bulgaria, with the emergence of Podkrepa in November 1989. Laws on strikes and disputes were an early feature of changes in the model of labour relations, as in Poland in 1982, Hungary in March 1989, Bulgaria in March 1990 and Czechoslovakia in early 1991.

Trade unionism has a number of features in relation to the transitional models of labour relations. First, their significance as agents in strategy formulation at both the national and enterprise levels. This relates to shifts in the relationships and the balance of forces between political and industrial interests. Secondly, their key role in interest representation, especially at the national political level, in a period when many new political parties are emerging and multiplying. Trade unions are organizations with mass memberships and claim to represent the interests not only of employees but also of other large sections of the population such as pensioners and the increasing numbers of unemployed. Przeworski (1991) argues that the role of trade unions in the process of economic reform is crucial because, on the one hand, they incorporate workers who are a potential source of wage pressure and hence of inflation; and on the other, through their centralized organizational features they can persuade their members to wait for various reforms to bear fruit. For these reasons, he argues, it is functionally necessary for labour unions to be centralized and all-encompassing. Thirdly, there are changes in the internal organization and functions of trade unions brought about by their formal separation from both party and state institutions. Solidarity in Poland, as the prototype of the independent alternative to the established unionism, was, in a sense, a social movement in that its goals were as much political as they were industrial. Since 1989 Solidarity has been faced with the dilemma of choosing between the specialized role of defending employee's interests in questions of wages, working conditions and employment and the more general role of "umbrella" for various post-Solidarity governments; that is, of taking joint responsibility for ruling the country (Morawski 1992b). In a similar fashion to Solidarity, the trade union alternatives established in Hungary and Bulgaria were also social movements in that they functioned at national and industrial levels because of their opposition to the Party and its affiliated unions. However, it is important to recognize that, in both Bulgaria and Hungary, initial support for these newly created unions was mainly concentrated in the non-manufacturing sectors of the economy. Hence they obtained their support among teachers, scientific workers and employees in areas of the health service. Underlying such patterns of "alternative" or "independent" support were the pre-revolutionary state socialist wage policies which gave priority to heavy manual work in productive industry rather than to the professional, non-productive activities undertaken by employees in the service sectors (Petkov & Thirkell 1991: 212–17).

No significant independent trade union movement has emerged in Russia, although some professional groups, such as airline pilots, have recognized their bargaining position and developed forms of collective organization (Clarke & Fairbrother 1993a: 91–120). In general, Russian trade unions have not emerged as an important political force in the process of economic change, either nationally or at enterprise level; they remain tainted as institutions associated with the past regime. Russian workers do not appear to conceive of independent trade unionism as a vehicle for mobilization. As Clarke (1993a: 24) comments: "The trade union within the enterprise was and is effectively a patronage network, integrated into and working alongside the management structure." However, for this reason, membership levels do not appear to have declined dramatically.

The advent of Solidarity in Poland and of political pluralism in Bulgaria and Hungary, and the challenges from alternative unions, have brought about changes in the organization, design and operation of the existing established union centres. This has led to their independence from the Communist Party, the end of democratic centralism as an organising principle, and the creation of confederal structures. In both Bulgaria and Hungary the reformed trade union centres have retained the largest membership (Thirkell et al. 1994; Hughes 1994). The duality of political and industrial functions of trade unionism relates to their operation at different levels of the economy: at the national political level, where decisions about macroeconomic policy are made; and at the enterprise level, where their members are employed. At the national level, the political function has been expressed mainly through tripartite forums. In specific political conditions, such as in Bulgaria in 1991–2, the national trade union confederations have operated as agencies of strategy formulation on major issues of economic policy, including the pace and content of measures for economic reform.

This national political role of trade unions has sometimes predominated over industry-level concerns, and this may help to explain the reduction of membership interest at the enterprise level. Linked to this there has often been an intermediating or "controlling" role, such as that of Solidarity, for example, in the Silesian mining dispute of 1992–3. Similarly in Bulgaria, the Confederation of Independent Trade Unions in Bulgaria (CITUB) has frequently been an agent of mediation in important disputes that have arisen in particular industries or enterprises. Such a role inevitably creates contradictions and tensions among rank-and-file members, since trade unions appear to function both as agents of government *and* as representatives of worker interests. This poses the question for trade unions of whether keeping governments in office is more important than representing rank-and-file demands, and whether there could be a "backlash" from members if redundancies increase and living standards fall. The experience of CITUB in Bulgaria suggests that although workers in specific sectors or enterprises may be dissatisfied with their conditions, the leading role of the trade union confederation as the chief agency for representing member interests has so far maintained a large measure of support. This is mainly because key decisions on minimum wages and the setting of budgets for social security – unemployment benefits and prices for key items such as food – are taken through negotiations and agreements at the national level.

Trade union density in socialist countries was extremely high, typically over 90 per cent. This was mainly because the availability of enterprise social funds for housing, holidays, kindergartens, transport and other social welfare benefits were distributed through the trade unions. Increases in unemployment, privatization programmes, especially of small service organizations, and the disappearance (except, at the time of writing, in the Czech and Slovak republics) of Social Funds is likely to lead to a reduction in union membership. In Poland, membership of both Solidarity and OPZZ appears to be in significant decline. However, figures for the Czech and Slovak republics suggest that this may not be inevitable (Brewster 1992). In addition, despite declines in Bulgaria and Hungary, membership of the confederations remains substantial.

Tripartism

It is clear from this discussion that there is a major difference between Russia and the eastern European countries with regard to the evolution of the trade union movement. This is also reflected in the development of tripartite forums which have been established in Bulgaria, the Czech and Slovak republics, Poland, Hungary and Russia. A number of questions arise in relation to the development of these: namely, the timing and the context in which the relevant institutions were established; the scope of issues covered; and their legal standing and degree of institutionalization. The prototype of a national tripartite council was created in Hungary in October 1988 while the Socialist Workers Party was still in government. A key agent in this process was the Research Institute of

Labour attached to the Ministry of Labour which contributed to the design of appropriate structures. The context for the establishment of tripartism was the process of economic reform emerging at this time, associated with increasing enterprise autonomy and some decentralization of control over wages, requiring the replacement of bureaucratic methods of wage determination by mechanisms more appropriate for a market economy (Héthy & Csuhaj 1990).

In Bulgaria, on the other hand, the National Commission created in February 1990 was the outcome of the economic crisis and industrial unrest that followed the political changes of November 1989. In January 1990 the reformed official trade unions (CITUB) demanded that the government should negotiate with them a General Agreement as a mechanism for securing political, economic and social consensus. Following the change of government in January 1990, a National Commission for the Reconciliation of Interests was established in order to negotiate this agreement. Thus, the CITUB was a leading agency in the creation of this structure and it also played a key role in the formation of an organization of state employers as the third party of tripartism.

The establishment of the Council for Czechoslovakia in the autumn of 1990 at the federal level was requested by the trade union confederation with the ready acquiescence of the government. The Council negotiated the first general agreement for the year 1991. In Poland, however, the creation of tripartite institutions was avoided until September 1992, although discussions of the relevance of a "corporatist" model had been common for several years. Hitherto, there had been informal and separate bipartite discussions between successive governments and the two confederations, Solidarity and OPZZ. Jacek Kuron, as Minister of Labour, was a leading agent in the process of trying to negotiate the state Enterprise Pact. This development took place against increasing strike pressure, which was only halted pending the outcome of the Pact, and evidence of widespread popular alienation from the political process (Tyszkiewicz 1992). In Russia a Federal Commission and some branch Tripartite Commissions were established at the end of 1991 and the beginning of 1992. The General Tripartite Agreement for 1993 is of a very general and all encompassing nature, being more of a list of preferred practices than a binding undertaking (Gerchikov, ch. 6 in this volume.)

Whether the range of issues covered by tripartite discussions is broad or narrowly defined depends largely upon the balance of power between governments and trade unions, and the socio-political context at specific periods of time. The most common area – with the exception of Russia – has been agreements on minimum and maximum wage increases, pensions, and the basis of wage indexation with relation to prices. This has been the case in Hungary since 1989, Bulgaria from 1990, and the Czech and Slovak republics after 1991. This will also be a key function of the Polish National Commission. The range of issues covered by tripartism has also broadened in these countries. In Hungary in 1991 and 1992, the National Council for the Reconciliation of Interests (NCRI) played a significant role in securing agreement on the social security provisions for the budget and in reform of the principles of enterprise taxation. In Slovakia towards the end of 1992, the main focus of discussions was the allocation of social expenditure from within the state budget: for example, unemployment benefits, food and transport subsidies and the rules for the Enterprise Social Fund, rather than upon the content of a General Agreement for 1993.

Issues of privatization are, of course, central to economic reforms. The great innovation of the Kuron Pact in Poland is the agreement for the involvement of trade unions in the process of privatization and the distribution of shares to workers. In Hungary, and the Czech and Slovak republics, privatization has been a governmental process operating outside both tripartite forums and negotiations with trade unions. In Bulgaria during the period of the coalition government (December 1990–October 1991), privatization was officially within the scope of the National Council, although it was not acted upon. The institutional status of tripartite forums varies. In Hungary, the National Council was given formal legal status by the Employment Act of 1991 and the Labour Code of 1992. In Bulgaria, the election of a coalition government in December 1990 to introduce price liberalization meant that the government was dependent on trade union support to maintain social peace. In these conditions the tripartite council operated as a standing body in which there was both consultation – typical of the period of the socialist government – and joint decision-making, with agreements binding on state organizations at lower levels. Of course, tripartism, by definition, requires organizations to represent the interests of employers. With the exception of Poland, where the Confederation of Polish Employers was established at the end of 1989, the development of employers' organizations has been related closely to the creation of tripartite institutions. Thus in Hungary in 1988, the already existing Chamber of the Economy became a partner in the National Council. In Bulgaria, the initiative for facilitating the organization of state employers in March 1990 came from the CITUB. Changes in the structure of property ownership brought about through privatization are obviously leading to a plurality of employers' organizations in different economic sectors, and the ease with which genuinely private employers can be incorporated into corporatist agreements is at this stage largely untested.

Collective bargaining

In all six countries, collective bargaining is a new feature of the transitional model and generally it is supported within a legal framework. The issues that arise relate to its coverage, to shifts in content from social welfare to wages, and to the legal framework as privatization proceeds. Contemporary discussions of collective bargaining tend to focus upon the negotiation of substantive collective agreements on terms and conditions at enterprise level. In the past, collective agreements at this level did not deal with terms and conditions of employment. There are many other issues such as the numbers and selection of employees for redundancy which may be the subject of collective bargaining by the trade unions, or of informal bargaining between individuals or work groups and line management (Thirkell & Tseneva 1992). There is legal provision for collective agreements at enterprise level in all of the countries, although the significance of this varies in accordance with national conditions. Understanding of the actual processes of negotiation at the enterprise level is constrained by a lack of survey data. However, the Czechoslovak Federal Research Institute of Labour and Social Affairs conducted a survey of collective bargaining and employee participation in 90 enterprises in mid-1991 (Cziria & Munkova 1991). This found that in 90 per cent of the enterprises collective agreements had been negotiated and, of these, 86 per cent were the result of trade union initiatives. In 1992, branch agreements were still used as a source of standards in the enterprises studied. In Bulgaria, the development of collective bargaining has been connected closely with initiatives from the National Tripartite Commission which issued Guidelines on Collective Bargaining in April 1990 and again in April 1991. In 1990, the coverage of workers by collective agreements was patchy and varied significantly between branches of industry.

Survey data on collective agreements in Bulgaria was compiled in November 1991 by the Confederation of Independent Trade Unions. The 1991 survey showed that by July 1991 only 37 per cent of state enterprises had negotiated collective agreements. The main stimulus to collective agreements came from the Decree on Wages and Collective Bargaining of 5 July 1991. This decree, which was passed in the context of the National Tripartite Agreement on Social Peace negotiated in June 1991, required collective agreements to be negotiated at enterprise level by September. This made enterprises the *only* level for collective agreements and thus removed the role of branches, except for the social sectors of health and education. The decree was accompanied by abolition of centralized control over enterprise wage funds based on the centrally determined wage rates for different grades of employee and the plan target for manpower. A national survey of 120 enterprises in November 1991 showed that 79 per cent of enterprises had signed agreements, and a further 14 per cent had completed the preparatory work (Thirkell & Tseneva 1992). In Poland, some branch agreements from the 1980s are still operative at the time of writing, although their significance is doubtful.

The development of wage bargaining in state enterprises has been tightly constrained by the high levels of taxation that have been levied on enterprises which allow wage increases. The creation of national machinery for wage negotiations in the state sector has been a major issue in the negotiations over the Kuron Pact. Private employers have been exempted from this taxation, but since they are mainly non-unionized there is no collective bargaining (Kozek 1993). It appears that current developments in collective bargaining in all the countries are primarily conditional upon the national mechanisms of economic management as applied to enterprises: for example, the tax mechanism in Poland and the 1991 Decree in Bulgaria. It is also clear that many new, small, privatized companies are outside the emerging model of collective bargaining.

Participation and consultation

The socialist enterprise has been conceptualized as having three internal vertical structures (Petkov & Thirkell 1991). The first was the structure of operational management; the second was the structure of the party and the trade union; and the third the structure of worker participation in management and/or "self management". The most usual institutions of the latter were a general assembly of employees (or of their representatives) and an elected council at the top of the enterprise. In the 1980s the general trend was to increase the scope and powers of this third structure and the empowerment of employees who were theoretically conceptualized as "co-owners". After the collapse of the old regimes there were two main questions to be considered at the political level. First, whether such institutions of the third structure needed to be preserved, destroyed or replaced. Secondly, what should the relationship be between institutions of participation and those of collective bargaining. The comparison between the countries of what has happened since the end of state socialism shows different patterns of development.

The Polish Enterprise Council of 1981 survived formally until the new provisions for the privatization of state enterprises. An initial stage was to transform the legal status of the enterprise into a "state treasury company", and for this the consent of the enterprise council was required. Once such a transfer is completed however, the enterprise council is dissolved so that the legal and institutional basis of participation disappears. In Russia the Council of the Labour Collective has also survived and it is required to agree plans for ownership change. However, in some enterprises the change to a joint stock company has been accompanied by the dissolution of the Labour Collective. It has sometimes been replaced by other enterprise councils, although the power of such bodies appears to be negligible. In Czechoslovakia, the State Enterprise Act of 1988, which included provisions for an enterprise council elected from the general assembly – that also elected the director – as a principal structure for participation, was repealed in May 1990. Its participative provisions were officially condemned as a "relic of socialism". Cziria and Munkova's survey showed that the provision of information and the process of consultation continued to occur in the majority of enterprises, but through trade union channels (Cziria & Munkova 1991). The Labour Code does not, however, prohibit the establishment of Works Councils and it is of interest to note that in two case study enterprises, managements set up Works Councils. In Bulgaria, the powers of the enterprise council were modified by Decree 56 of 1988. The Labour Code was revised at the end of 1992 after negotiations between successive governments and the trade union confederations had continued since 1990. This provided for the general assembly of employees to elect representatives to decide questions of enterprise management, but did not specify any structure or mechanisms for this. In Hungary, the Labour Code of 1992 covering employees participative rights replaced the previous enterprise councils with Works Councils. It sets out in detail the provisions for these, which are required in every firm or establishment with more than 50 employees, although the rights are mainly consultative. In both Bulgaria and Hungary the issue of the relationship between the institutions of participation and those of collective bargaining have been the subject of dispute between the government and the trade union confederations. In the former, towards the end of 1991, the newly elected government of the Union of Democratic Forces proposed that a revised Labour Code should provide for a Works Council which would be the bargaining agent for the collective agreement rather then the trade union. Similarly, in the initial drafts of the Hungarian Labour Code, the government sought to make the Works Council the bargaining agent, but in Hungary, as in Bulgaria, the trade unions were successful in resisting the government's proposals.

Thus the previous rights of employees to participate in management have been eroded significantly in the transitional models. In socialist theory, employees were co-owners of the state property of their enterprises. Now, however, in all countries there are varying forms of provision for employee share ownership so that they have possibilities for some financial participation as shareholders in their privatized enterprises. The evidence from some Polish enterprises suggests that workers are willing to accept routes to privatization which destroy workplace mechanisms of participation because privatization is presented as the economic salvation of enterprises and therefore also of employment, and accordingly strategies of survival predominate at company level. Solidarity as a national organization is committed to the consolidation of single channel representation in which the trade union is the sole bargaining agent at enterprise level. Trade unions have been prepared to concede the dilution of mechanisms of employee participation in management because they have been concerned to secure and consolidate their position as the sole bargaining agent in collective bargaining. Hungary is exceptional in that Works Councils are constituted legally. However, the elections to Works Councils in May 1993 demonstrated that in many enterprises the trade unions were successful in securing the election of their own candidates on these bodies.

In general, we can say that changes in Labour Codes, which provide the framework for a reform of collective bargaining, have acted as "anticipatory frameworks", in the sense of the attempt to devise a system appropriate for a market economy *before* that economy exists (Thompson & Smith 1992). In Western capitalist countries, labour law more typically has developed organically or pragmatically in response to emerging labour relations configurations. By contrast, pre-emptive labour legislation in eastern Europe may serve to structure and limit the possibilities of development at enterprise level. Offe makes a similar point about the problems of simultaneity in trying to create a constitution, a democratic process and "normal politics" in one operation: "As a consequence the decisions made on all three of these levels may easily turn out to be incompatible so as to obstruct each other rather than forming a coherent whole" (Offe 1991).

At the enterprise level, labour relations are affected, obviously, by emerging managerial strategies, with these, in turn, being shaped by three main factors. First, a central condition for a large number of enterprises in eastern Europe has been the disintegration of the Soviet market which was traditionally a major outlet for production, organized through COMECON (Council for Mutual Economic Assistance). In these conditions, business strategy, in the sense of seeking to maintain a share of existing markets or to find new ones, has become a major issue for the management of many enterprises. In particular instances the market crisis has been so acute that the future of an enterprise has been threatened and the central task of management has been to attempt to devise a survival strategy by whatever means possible. This can be through short-time working or even by keeping workers on payrolls but without wages. In production industries, the general picture is one of managements trying, with varying degrees of success, to find new markets in the West or elsewhere. This process sometimes involves joint ventures; alternatively, it has included trying to maintain some part of the former Soviet markets, often through complex barter deals. The second factor is that privatization is the officially declared objective of all governments and, at enterprise level, ownership change can present management with threats, in the form of external financial controls, or opportunities, such as investment for improved technology, and, in some cases, chances to secure substantial blocs of shares. In situations where there is an opportunity for employees to obtain shares in their enterprises, privatization may affect labour relations by changing the status of at least some employees. The prospect of ownership change, sometimes combined with the search for new markets, has led frequently to a third form of change:

that is, the internal restructuring of enterprises, initiated by top management. This has often resulted in increases in the operational autonomy of enterprise-owned plants, workshops and departments. Although enterprise restructuring *before* privatization is common it can also occur *after* privatization, for example, when the ownership of different parts of the enterprise is broken up. All these changes have implications for labour relations and may trigger or constrain management's articulation of labour relations strategy.

Conclusions

A general point is that emerging institutions are fragile, precarious and unstable. The absence, presence or threat of pressure from employees has been a major condition for institutional development and change. The different routes from Communist Party domination, involving either capitulation, compromise or electoral competition, persist in affecting the emerging labour relations models in the countries studied; this is notwithstanding the common pattern of ideological influences from abroad and the encouragement of Western models of social partnership and the social market model of corporatism. Not surprisingly, governments have viewed the development of new labour relations institutions as secondary to economic reform and privatization.

The role of trade unions in the immediate aftermath of the collapse of communist regimes seems to vary from country to country. Arguably, they have been a driving force of social and political change in Poland and Bulgaria. In the Czech and Slovak republics, reform has been more consensual, whereas in Hungary governments have taken a more positive lead role. In Russia the historical image of the trade unions has not encouraged workers to view independent trade unionism as a potential force for representing their interests. Despite these differences, however, trade unions in all the countries have been orientated towards the state as the agent of reform. Trade unions are compelled to act on the national political stage since their demands cannot be pursued solely at the enterprise level. In the past, trade union control of the social funds of enterprises provided the pay-back for individual membership. Now that social security and benefits are no longer primarily provided by enterprises, these issues have shifted to the national political stage. Trade unions in these countries claim to represent not only the employed, but also the unemployed and pensioners, in national negotiations over social fund and social security issues. This may help to explain the tendency for trade union membership levels to decline, since the pay-off for individual membership has changed. If the focus is national agreements, the individual at enterprise level can free-ride on tripartite agreements without needing to belong to a trade union. However, in Russia, the persistence of a trade union role in enterprise-based patronage systems may have served to maintain membership levels, if not active participation by members. In the other countries, the salience of national economic issues and tripartite negotiations have limited the development of trade union functions at both branch and enterprise levels. If corporatist arrangements fail and are discredited, the legitimacy of trade unions can be compromised. Thus trade unions can run the risk of becoming once again "transmission belts", but this time for government austerity measures.

In all the countries – with the possible exception of Russia – tripartism or corporatism has arisen as a government response to the real or perceived threat of political and industrial instability. Trade unions are a major basis for consensus building and legitimation in a context where political parties are weak and fragmented. Governments have faced choices between the alternative strategies of confirming and strengthening tripartite institutions, or of seeking to avoid them (Héthy 1991). The evidence shows that up to the mid-1990s in Hungary and the Czech and Slovak republics there has been an incremental development of tripartism. The Kuron Pact initiative in Poland was motivated by industrial unrest, but prior to that, the fact that Solidarity was already enmeshed with the government may have obviated the need for formal corporatist arrangements. In Bulgaria, the government tried to extricate itself from tripartism in 1992 but was successful only for a short time.

The crucial future issue for corporatism in these countries is whether tripartite agreements are substantively underwritten. Can the parties to political exchange deliver their sides of the bargains? Experience from western Europe would suggest that corporatism needs delivery mechanisms at lower levels; for example, collective bargaining structures or works councils must be capable of relaying interest intermediation to enterprise level (Crouch 1992). Certainly in Russia the institutions for such intermediation are largely absent. This suggests that the degree to which corporatist arrangements may be articulated from national to enterprise levels is of critical importance. In relation to this process of articulation there are a number of potential problems. First, the weakness of employers' association questions whether trade unions or governments will be able to make agreements enforceable, as an increasing proportion of employment is located in both private and small-scale organizations in which union membership is likely to be low or nonexistent. Secondly, can trade unions intermediate their members' interests successfully without losing rank and file support, especially if economic restructuring programmes prevent governments from delivering social benefits?

As discussed earlier, collective bargaining or collective agreements have been incorporated within the labour legislation of all the countries. These represent a "top-down" approach which raises the question of the likelihood of collective agreements being implemented at the level of the enterprise. There are several factors that may influence this. Evidence from Bulgaria suggests that the major impetus for the development of collective agreements can emerge from the outcome of national tripartite negotiations – as was the case in 1991 when these were drafted in a form which provided for explicit articulation from the national level down to the level of the enterprise. Similarly, the development of enterprise collective agreements in Czechoslovakia in 1990–1 was dependent partly on the content of the national General Agreement, although this articulation was not backed by legal requirements. At this time the enterprises were state property so that the state at national level could instruct, if necessary, state managers at enterprise level to implement the agreements. As the process of privatization proceeds, the issue of collective bargaining at lower levels becomes an issue of strategy by managers who are no longer state employees. It is clear from the experience of Poland, and the Czech and Slovak republics, that in small firms in the retail, trading and service sector, employers frequently do not recognize trade unions and consequently there is no collective bargaining (Kozek 1993). The prospects for collective bargaining in larger enterprises as they are privatized remains uncertain. Whether these employers will seek to withdraw from collective agreements will depend upon the contingent conditions such as the strength of union organization in the enterprise, and the influence of the union externally – and especially on the nature and coverage of national tripartite agreements. In relation to the latter, much will depend on the development or decline of industrial conflict and on the perceptions of the prospect for social peace.

Collective bargaining through trade unions has provided one channel of representation; employee or Works Councils can provide a second. However, as discussed above, only Hungary has legal provisions for works councils and has thus formalized dual channel representation. In Poland, the processes of privatization are leading to the elimination of the old employee councils, a process not mourned by Solidarity trade unions who want trade unions to be the sole channel or representative. An interesting test of the importance attached by employees as well as trade unions to such mechanisms took place in Hungary in May 1993, when the provisions of the Labour Code relating to the election of Works Councils members came into effect. In practice, unions were generally able to secure the election of their members to the councils and the success of unions affiliated to the National Association of Hungarian Trade Unions (MSZOSZ) was generally much greater than that of the more recently formed unions. Thus, although there are clear differences between the Labour Codes in the different countries with regard to participation mechanisms, in practice trade unions remain the most significant channel for worker representation at enterprise level. Nevertheless, the pre-emptive nature of the new Labour Codes may serve to limit or constrain more organic developments in the future.

At enterprise level there is growing evidence that senior management may seize the opportunity to dismiss or ignore participative mechanisms. In case studies conducted in companies in Russia and Poland there are examples of Directors operating outside the legislation or on the borders of legality: for example, in Poland in advance of ownership change disestablishing the Employee Council, and in Russia, using changes in ownership as a chance to get rid of the Council of the Labour Collective (Kozek et al., ch.5 in this volume; Gerchikov, ch. 6 in this volume). This reinforces the importance of enterprise level strategy and the developing role of management. The relative autonomy of the enterprise and the scope for the development of enterprise strategies will remain a critical element in the emerging labour relations models.

Clearly, an important factor shaping the character of corporatism and of labour relations models is the changing role of the state, which in turn is shaped by conjunctures of different political forces. In all the east European countries, political processes remain semi-structured as numerous competing political parties struggle to mobilize popular support. The absence of *dominant* parties of the kind found in Western countries results in weakened political legitimacy, with the effect that the role of

28

the state as an *ideological* integrative mechanism is underdeveloped. This strengthens the appeal of corporatism as a means of securing political consent, although the degree of popular support for this is uncertain. Even so, state institutions remain highly influential within the countries of eastern Europe because of their functions in the provision of health, education and welfare, as well as other economically productive services. As yet the nature of state institutions and how these are likely to emerge within ongoing programmes of privatization is unclear, but undoubtedly it will have outcomes for the character of tripartism and the role of labour relations models. Without the emergence of political mobilization, competing political parties and the construction of highly legitimized state institutions, social pacts incorporating the interests of both workers and corporate owners are likely to remain unstable.

The outcome of the current wave of tripartism will certainly play a key role, and the level and manner of articulation of bargains will help to structure the relationships between the different levels of labour relations: the national, the branch and the enterprise. Perhaps the most interesting question, and the most difficult to answer, is the extent to which current developments, especially in the field of privatization, may be foreclosing certain labour relations approaches or options for the future. The explanation of developments will come from the comparison of processes in countries and this will facilitate the mapping of alternative scenarios, in which the counter-factual – what does *not* happen – will be as significant and as interesting as what does. However, the purpose of this volume is to offer an introduction to the changes that are occurring in labour relations within the differing circumstances of Bulgaria, the Czech and Slovak republics, Hungary, Poland and Russia. Only upon such a descriptive basis is it possible to search for explanations that account for similarities and differences within the fundamental societal transformations confronting the countries of central and eastern Europe.

CHAPTER 2
Bulgaria

Krastyu Petkov and Grigor Gradev

There are two major aims to this chapter: to describe the development of industrial relations in Bulgarian enterprises, and to discuss the contextual pressures, influences and interdependencies accompanying the process of transformation of society. Both of these have helped to shape emerging workplace industrial relations systems. The empirical information on which this chapter is based has been collected for over two years, starting in April 1992, in four enterprises from different branches of industry. The cases are shown in Table 2.1. In addition, data from other studies of industrial relations and economic reforms have been used, together with surveys and national statistics.

The selection of particular enterprises for the case studies was a difficult task under the conditions in Bulgaria, because the anticipated process of privatization has been repeatedly delayed. After an intensive process of searching and consultations with government bodies, a list of possible cases was prepared. Although Bos Air was in the first list of en-

Table 2.1 Bulgarian enterprises: a profile of four case study enterprises.

Enterprise	FLEX TOOL	BOS AIR	FERROMOULD	STARTCOM
Branch	Hand tools, motors	Air transport	Foundry	Electric motors
Number of employees	1992: 1,500	1993: 4,000	1990: 350 1992: 600	1991; 1,800
Ownership status	Joint-stock company – state owned	State owned	Joint venture, then state controlled	State owned

terprises to be privatized, this process has still not been completed. Flex Tool and Startcom have not even started and Ferromould, with a large private shareholding at the beginning of the study, underwent a process of increasing state control. All the enterprises are former state firms that under legislation have been transformed into limited companies such as Startcom and Bos Air, or as a joint stock company for example Flex Tool. However, the state remains the only owner of shares or stocks, although the change opens up important new possibilities for decision-making, which facilitates the process of privatization. The fourth enterprise, Ferromould, became a joint venture between the state (40 per cent) and Western capital (60 per cent).

Flex Tool   The company was transformed in May 1993 into a joint-stock company with the state being the only stockholder. Flex Tool was created originally through co-operation with the German-owned AEG, which continued until 1986. The company is currently working on two product lines: hand tools, and motors for the assembly of tools. The quality is good for the comparatively low prices charged and the company has always been export-orientated. In tools production, Flex Tool has a virtual monopoly in the country and it enjoyed a similar position within eastern Europe. In 1992 the production of motors was halted but it resumed at the end of 1993. Apart from COMECON, Flex Tool's main interests are directed towards the Western market: Europe, Latin America, South Korea and South-east Asia. It conducts its export activities through a state foreign trade company, and through it, it is linked to joint companies for distribution in France, Germany and Poland. The strategy of the company is to develop direct links with the markets. The General Director was replaced in 1992, allegedly for attempting, with a German partner, to privatize the company. In 1992 Flex Tool was included in the privatization list but was later taken out. The workforce of Flex Tool is about 1,500 people, of whom at least two-thirds are in the production shops. Despite the growth of market pressures, Flex Tool has survived with few cuts in the workforce. Work is organized in two shifts, and based upon the brigade system. The enterprise is currently embarking on an ambitious programme to increase production in 1994.

Startcom   This company was established in the late 1960s to manufacture components for the expanding car industry in the former Soviet Union, but later extended its product range to parts for CNC machines, robots, electronic automation systems and electric motors for industrial and home use. Up to 97 per cent of its production was destined for the Soviet market, but in the 1990s there has been a remarkable reorientation to Western markets and a rapid contraction of sales to Russia. The company is structured according to four profit-and-loss centres, each for a separate product. It also participates in two joint ventures, with Italian and American distributors. The General Director was replaced in the autumn of 1992. About 1,800 people work for Startcom and cuts in the workforce were insignificant until 1993, when market conditions prompted the need for restructuring and reduction of the workforce.

Bos Air   This company came into being as a result of a strike in the former state-owned consortium in 1991. This was split into ten independent companies, with Bos Air as the largest and practically the only provider of passenger and cargo services. International services are the major business and although the quality of service is not at the level of that of Western competitors, prices are considerably lower and this attracts transit passengers. It is a large company by eastern European standards, with about 40 aircraft and 4,000 employees. Recently it has modernized its fleet by leasing from Western companies. The financial position of the company is deteriorating, although there is an increase in passenger numbers: this is one of the major reasons why it is being considered for privatization. The involvement of a large foreign investor is considered to be a life saving strategy for Bos Air that will help turn it into a modern, competitive airline company. Most of the procedures for privatization are completed, but the process is cumbersome and, in 1993, after almost reaching completion, a new proposal was put forward by the Agency for Privatization. It is expected that about 1,000 employees will be made redundant after privatization.

Ferromould   This was a joint venture that was conceived during the politically turbulent period of 1990–1. It took over trading from a former state company that in 1990 was facing closure, and it rented most of its premises and equipment. The products of Ferromould were garden seats, gully-hole covers, counterweights for washing machines, etc. This was below the potential of the technology which had previously produced engine blocks. The aim was to expand the earlier trading links of the enterprise and establish it as a strong force in the home market. At the time of writing Ferromould has no problems with orders from abroad.

The company employed 350 people at first and the number increased to 600 in 1992. It paid the highest wages in the region. Foreign investment in the business was because of future privatization plans, but because of delays backers have withdrawn their interest, leaving behind substantial debts and workers without salaries. In the mid-1990s, the enterprise has almost returned to its former state-owner and, while it is still in operation, its future is unclear.

The context: privatization and strategy formulation

The analysis in this chapter is based on the understanding that the processes and events characterizing industrial relations in the period (known as the "transition to market economy and pluralist society") develop under the influence or direct pressure of a number of factors operating at two levels of structure – the national and the workplace. The internal process of change at each level derives from interaction with external factors and there is some dependence between the two levels. Thus, the process of change at the workplace, for example on privatization, will depend on the legal changes at the national level, which in turn depend on the balance of political power. A framework for the chapter is set out in Figure 2.1.

Legal regulation is crucial for legitimating new concepts and for setting the standards and norms which form the basis of the system, the law on collective labour disputes, and other regulations influencing wages and social benefits, as well as the commercial and privatization laws. In Bulgaria the development of legal regulation has been a contentious issue dependent upon the political process which, since 1989, has been very turbulent. Thus, the Labour Code was only revised at the end of 1992 and ownership transformation has been delayed repeatedly. The interaction between economic reform and the political process has also been an uneven one. Since 1990, the international financial agencies have been extremely active in Bulgaria and seeking to influence the government policies for economic reform. The ILO has been concerned with advising on the promotion of social dialogue, and ways of developing the industrial relations system. Established social and cultural assumptions, such as the egalitarian value system, have an influence on the events in some of the case studies, although their precise effect is difficult to determine.

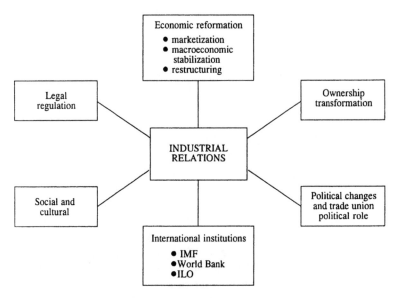

Figure 2.1 A framework for industrial relations in Bulgaria.

New and old structures

Within this framework the chapter explores the interaction between old and new structures, and the degree of continuity and discontinuity in the process of transformation. After the dramatic political events in eastern Europe in the autumn of 1989 it was expected that the transition to a market economy and pluralistic society would take a relatively short time. These ideas and expectations, despite some initial successes, turned out to be largely over-optimistic given the complex situation of Bulgaria. Changes in industrial relations were developing even under the old regime. In the workplace, tensions had been increasing since the middle of the 1980s, and industrial stoppages had occurred for the first time in decades. In 1989, a new trade union, Podkrepa was formed, and although immediately forced underground by the authorities, this could not remove the challenge to the system. Voices for defending the rights and interests of working people began to be raised in the established unions as well. The political shifts in 1989 created opportunities for open political debate, and trade unions immediately took the initiative. Industrial rela-

35

tions gained their own momentum but they were still heavily dependent on the progress of change in other areas of reform. The start of the process can be found in a number of the structures from the different reforms of the 1980s, corresponding to pieces of legislation, especially the Labour Code, which was designed for worker self- management. In the period 1990–2 coexistence of the self-management bodies – General Assemblies and Assemblies of Delegates, and the administrative bodies of management and the Boards of Directors – were quite common in enterprises. With the removal of the pressure for centralized political control, self-managing structures were not only revitalized but also for the first time enjoyed real autonomy of action. This definitely shifted the power balance in their favour and they immediately began to execute their rights and to reshape the enterprise and its relations within this environment. For example, decisions could be taken to declare enterprises to be independent entities and to withdraw from the large, state-owned consortia. This started a process of organic restructuring, leading towards decentralization of the economy. Further, directors could be replaced without national campaigns for elections, as in 1986. At the same time, changes were introduced in the course of industrial conflicts, when strike committees appeared as new power centres competing with old union and managerial structures. Quite often these committees provided the core for new union organizations in enterprises by ousting the leadership of the old unions and re-establishing them on a reformed basis. The first new trade union structure – Podkrepa – grew very quickly, while the older unions had to go through a difficult process of internal reforms. It took the newly created CITUB a longer time to gain public legitimacy.

Political reforms

Political changes have exerted a strong influence in the field of industrial relations; they have both facilitated and blocked the social dialogue. Policies towards labour relations have varied between governments and there have been considerable shifts during the terms of different governments. Trade unions have tried to play an active role and provide proposals, but final decisions have been a government responsibility. Trade unions were present at round table talks in the spring of 1990 that attempted to define the future direction for the transformation of society.

36

Subsequently they have been party to national agreements, or initiators of protest actions that have been instrumental in the survival or fall of governments. Characteristic features of post-communist Bulgaria are the uncertainty of executive power and frequent political crises, which have limited the scope and the depth of reforms. In the course of less than four years there were five governments.

Immediately after the first elections of June 1990, the Bulgarian Communist Party, later the Socialist Party, retained power. This government tried to avoid confrontation with the unions in order to buy time for changing the Party and it soon entered into negotiations with CITUB which were joined later by Podkrepa. The government was then brought down by a national strike initiated by Podkrepa and later supported by CITUB. The coalition government that came to power had a favourable attitude towards unions and recognized the significance of social dialogue in the success of reforms. Following a national political agreement and the recommendations of the IMF it signed an agreement for social peace with the trade unions and applied the "shock therapy" approach as the major means for macroeconomic stabilization. The success of this monetarist strategy and the duration of the coalition government was short-lived. After new elections in October 1991 a neo-liberal government of the Union of Democratic Forces (UDF) was formed. Since Podkrepa has been a major power block within UDF it felt privileged at the beginning and CITUB was openly discriminated against and attacked. The government fell in the autumn of 1992 because of strong pressures by both trade unions. The next government was made up of "experts" without clear political support. During its first steps it reinstated institutionalized social dialogue through the new Labour Code at the beginning of 1993. Later, the early thrust for co-operation faded and industrial relations were marked by growing tensions. Initially, industrial relations and trade unions had been viewed as secondary and supportive elements in the process of socio-political transformation, but actual developments demonstrated their key role as channels for democracy and reform.

Economic reforms

Compared to the other eastern European countries, economic reform in Bulgaria started quite late and its active lifespan was quite short. It followed the logic of the neo-classical, monetarist approach and started in the beginning of 1991, but before the end of that summer the reform effort lost momentum. A major characteristic of the Bulgarian variant has been the restitution of nationalized properties (including land) which was carried out before the privatization of state and municipal properties. Bulgaria is the only country in eastern Europe with systematic restitution legislation – nine laws passed by the mid-1990s and some drafts still to come. As a result, a whole social stratum has appeared of owners with considerable resources that could be used in privatization. The economic reforms inevitably have a liberal character and comprise, so far, three processes of macroeconomic stabilization, marketization, and restructuring. Macroeconomic stabilization began in February 1991. It included a package of measures such as liberalization of prices, restrictive wage and incomes policy, high interest rates, and tight control on credit. After a year of stagnation and mass shortages of goods and services in 1990, the nature of the processes that developed in the Bulgarian economy did not differ from those in other countries in eastern Europe. The disintegration of COMECON seriously impaired the functioning of Bulgarian economy and placed it in a situation of isolation. The economy has been export-orientated, mostly to the former Soviet Union (about 80 per cent) and eastern Europe, with only 4–6 per cent to the West. This sudden interruption of economic relations left many enterprises with unsaleable production, cancelled agreements and exhausted credit. There was the problem of "bad debts", which has had a constraining effect even on profitable enterprises and which became a major obstacle to their privatization. In these conditions survival was the main problem for enterprises, and survival strategies had to be formulated by them without assistance from higher levels.

Production levels declined by 40 per cent in 1990, 28 per cent in 1991, and 15 per cent in 1992, accompanied by attempts to reduce costs – wages, social payments, and investment in new technology and infrastructure. However, unemployment did not grow at a corresponding rate until 1992–3 when those officially registered as jobless reached 16 per cent, and a household survey by the State Statistical Institute indicated 21 per cent at the end of 1993. In general, enterprises have been left on their own to survive and this has exerted strong pressure for deregulation. Government policy towards de-monopolization has been aimed at creating independent economic units and the end of state subsidies, but the state still collects 70–80 per cent of enterprise profit through the tax system. However, the most successful companies have been those that have entered into joint ventures with foreign firms and gained direct access to international markets, as is the case with Flex Tool and Startcom. Another relevant enterprise strategy has been to produce in collaboration with customers and suppliers. Despite initial changes, the Russian market now continues to play a key role for Bulgarian enterprises, and some companies are renewing previous links. For many, privatization is considered to be the only viable alternative. But even so, until 1993 only about 3–4 major privatization projects have been completed.

Ownership transformation

Various models were considered in 1990–1 with different political parties and other interest groups putting forward proposals for privatization. A common feature of these was a concern for the social consequences and the need for mass participation. Both trade union confederations supported this approach. There was also "small-scale" privatization during this period with the transfer of small properties – shops and workshops – to private owners. This process was later terminated by Parliament since there was a tendency to degrade it to one almost of making gifts on the basis of political or kinship factors. In 1991 the Agency for Privatization was set up, which developed its own regional network, trained specialists and started the first privatization procedures. During this same period most of the state enterprises were transformed into joint-stock companies or limited liability companies but with the state as the sole owner. In 1992 Parliament passed a Law for Privatization and started discussions on a national privatization programme. In Bulgaria there is considerable flexibility as to the methods and techniques of privatization. As a legal norm, the procedure can be initiated in a number of ways, including management of the enterprise, the employees or potential outside investors. The crucial feature of privatization in Bulgaria is the delay in implementation and the conflict that raged in 1993 between the government and the Agency for Privatization for the control over state enterprises. In 1993 the Council of Ministers twice dismissed the supervisory Board of the Agency and each time the Supreme Court reinstated it. This caused further delay. One result, however, is that this led to the advance of "hidden" privatization and the growth of unregistered business enterprises. In 1993 mass privatization was brought to the fore again by the government, with its plans to privatize about 300 enterprises through the distribution of vouchers to the adult population. The main trade unions are critical about privatization but they do not oppose it. CITUB is especially sceptical of the project for mass privatization and has its own proposals for facilitating the process. One of its proposals is for employee share ownership and management buy-outs.

Enterprise strategies

All our case studies were selected as having the potential to survive, to adapt and to formulate new strategies for development, but over time their position shifted significantly. Flex Tool suffered considerably from the demise of the COMECON system. But at the same time, liberalization of prices and the floating exchange rate of the dollar largely compensated for any losses. Its major strategy in 1992 was to establish a presence in new markets in the West, the Far East and other regions, to wait for opportunities to restore links in the Russian market and to develop direct relations with customers which avoided the use of intermediaries. A year later Flex Tool revived its motor production for Russia, recorded its first successes in market diversification and entered into negotiations with Macedonia, the Arab Emirates and Venezuela, with a view to starting joint ventures. Until the middle of 1993 privatization was not considered to be an issue at Flex Tool. Management was even concerned that the offer from large Western companies to buy were motivated by a desire to close it in order to take over its markets. As a result, management chose the alternative of continuing state ownership and employee share ownership to secure the control of the company; this strategy persists to the present time.

Startcom is the most successful example of a company using traditional links with the Soviet Union for the purposes of adaptation and also for reorientating enough of its business towards Western markets. Privatization is recognized as one of the key drivers for defining future product and technology innovation, and market expansion. There is foreign interest in acquiring enterprises but management has preferred a situation where the state, management and employees share ownership.

Bos Air has been engaged in lengthy negotiations about privatization.

Proposals began in 1993 and were approaching the final stages when, at the end of the year, these were changed by the Agency and approved by the government. The new scheme was definitely in favour of local participants. Bulgarian institutions and individuals will hold a minimum of 51 per cent of the capital. The state will keep 40 per cent and the employees can take up to 20 per cent at preferential rate.

Ferromould is the company with the most developed and most sophisticated strategies. It is the result of the collaboration of Western and Bulgarian managers, who are well aware of potential opportunities. The declared aim is to privatize the factory through foreign ownership. However, this strategy underestimated local interests and the potential of unions to mobilize support for industrial relations issues. These created a powerful block which engaged the enterprise in constant conflict with the workforce. As a result, the enterprise closed down and was later taken over by a Bulgarian manager.

Trade union responses

Trade unions were the first to take advantage of the change in the political situation in 1989. Their changes were faster, and the organizations became orientated to the new situation and exploited opportunities more efficiently than did the political parties. The earliest developments in Bulgaria were similar to those in other eastern European countries: a parallel operation of new trade union structures along with the old ones at national, local and enterprise levels. These similarities were largely reproduced in the nature of the organizations, the character of their activities, and the aims and means employed. New trade union structures had significant advantages in the conditions of change, mainly in two directions. First, they were born with the idea of change and therefore pretend to be the "gurus" and the "motors" of transformation. Secondly, their lack of previous activities permitted considerable freedom in establishing a favourable public image, with purity of motivation, "trust" and the message of freedom and democracy. The first new trade union organization in Bulgaria was the Confederation of Labour Podkrepa and it combined skilfully all favourable factors into a two-pronged strategy: the immediate demolition of the communist social and political system, with industrial action being the major tool; and the defence of the real interests of union members and workers. This dual strategy was formulated and publicly expressed in very strong anti-communist rhetoric. Podkrepa enjoyed a strong response from working people and especially from the intellectual professions. The organization grew at a rapid rate and reported a membership of 100,000 in March 1990. It was not large but was extremely active and powerful, which confirmed the effectiveness of its strategy during that period. Podkrepa adopted the hegemonic aspiration of becoming the only representative of labour in industrial relations. Combined with its ideas for demolition of the established system and a fast growing membership – much larger than any other newly created political organization except for CITUB – Podkrepa became an extremely powerful as both a political and an industrial force. This duality in the nature of Podkrepa served it efficiently in the beginning, but with time it became a problem. Podkrepa was one of the founder members of the Union of Democratic Forces (UDF), the major political challenger to the Communist Party, (later named the Bulgarian Socialist Party). This situation led to tensions over the use of trade union structures for political purposes and the problems of identity with other trade unions.

The older established trade union organization faced a strategic choice of a quite difficult nature. If it were to survive, it would be necessary to undergo a total internal reform and to start defending the immediate interests of the workers. The pressure from below erupted in hundreds of industrial conflicts which were accompanied by spontaneous decisions by workers to leave. The other urgent change concerned relations with political organizations. The establishment trade unions soon declared their independence from the Communist Party (Petkov & Thirkell 1991), although this placed them in an isolated position, since new political parties considered them to be "hidden" communist forces. The established unions re-formed themselves as the new Confederation of Independent Trade Unions (CITUB) in February 1990. CITUB's position was that the efficient working of democratic structures and mechanisms in industrial relations would contribute more to the transformation of the economy and society. CITUB has remained the organization with the largest membership, with members of different political opinions.

Collective bargaining has become established as the core of the activity of workplace trade unionism in the period of transformation, although until 1993 trade union structures were used for the solution of other problems at the enterprise. They were engaged in some unusual activities, such as the restructuring of older, larger companies and initiating changes in management, and, most important, the replacement of directors. (In 1991 and 1992 about 2,000 directors were replaced.)

Social partnership

Each government has formulated its own policy towards trade unions and this has meant different approaches to tripartism. However, the idea came from CITUB at the beginning of 1990, when the Communist Party was still in power, and when the country was in a constant state of industrial unrest. In March, the Law for Collective Labour Disputes was adopted by Parliament with the agreement of CITUB and the level of strikes declined. The first General Agreement between CITUB, the government and the emerging organization of employers – only state employees at that time – was signed and included most issues of concern, including mechanisms for indexation of wage increases and collective bargaining in the workplace. The reaction of Podkrepa was strongly negative and CITUB was presented as collaborator of the communist government for the preservation of the old regime, but a month later Podkrepa joined the General Agreement. Relations between the social partners were marked by growing tension and this led to the necessity for new negotiations in September 1990 and a new General Agreement. Podkrepa declared a national strike and when later CITUB joined it the government was forced to resign. The next government was difficult to form because after the first free elections in June 1990 the Bulgarian Socialist Party had gained a majority in Parliament. In search of a solution based on consensus politics, a coalition government was formed but this lacked support in Parliament. Its main task was to introduce monetarist economic reforms. One of the first steps of the new government in 1991 was to secure the co-operation of the trade unions. An Agreement for Social Peace was signed, which later led to the creation of the National Tripartite Commission and the official recognition of tripartism as policy-making tool. The Commission had powers to resolve industrial relations and social security issues, with its decisions being binding on the government. The main targets of macroeconomic stabilization were achieved after the first six months, although during this period inflation rocketed to over 600 per cent and living standards fell 40–45 per cent but there were no major industrial conflicts or civil unrest. Political conditions were sufficiently favourable for further reforms – restructuring and privatization. This, however, created internal frictions which rendered the government incapable of continuing with reforms. New elections in October 1991 brought to power the first non-communist government – the United Democratic Front. It had most seats in Parliament but not an overall majority. The new government was of a neo-liberal nature, with strong anti-union policies. It was not interested in social partnership and it ignored the role of tripartite bodies and trade unions. The government fell late in 1992 to be replaced by a new "government of experts" which took office but without clear political support. From the beginning of 1993 industrial relations were subject to a revised version of the Labour Code, and tripartism was institutionalized at national, industrial and regional levels. The Labour Code and the accompanying normative acts provided the framework for the system of industrial relations appropriate for the period of transformation. The National Council for Tripartite Collaboration (NCTC) was set up to regulate issues of wage policy, living standards, pensions, taxation, unemployment benefits and child allowances. The decisions of the Council are taken by consensus and each party undertakes the necessary steps to implement decisions. The Labour Code defines the criteria for representative organizations, which include no less than 50,000 members from a spread of different industries. About a dozen organizations have applied for representation in NCTC but only two have been admitted – CITUB and Podkrepa. Recognition is important because it carries automatic recognition for all members for collective bargaining in the workplace. After several months of comparatively successful collaboration, the work of NCTC came under increasing criticism from unions, especially CITUB. The main accusation was that NCTC has been used by the government as a "front". As a result, CITUB led a successful national miners' strike in December 1993 and Podkrepa declared, but later cancelled, a national strike against the government in February 1994.

Employers organizations

A distinctive feature of tripartism in this period of transformation is the lack of real employer structures (ILO-CEET 1994). This usually reduces tripartism to bipartism – between the trade unions and the state. The first employers' organization appeared in 1990, curiously through the assistance of CITUB in its effort to establish social partnership. State employers, as they were at that time, proved to be unrepresentative and the organization was soon left outside the tripartite process. With time, new employer organizations appeared, but all with somewhat unclear character and policy. Because of the delay of privatization, they have all been linked to the state. The first to shape itself as an autonomous entity was the Economic Chamber, which includes some new private businesses but still consists of mainly state owned enterprises. The other organization of a similar nature is the Bulgarian Trade and Industrial Chamber, which later joined the tripartite arrangements. Other organizations have appeared for the purpose of protecting the interests of smaller businesses. The Union for Entrepreneurial Initiatives of Citizens was founded in 1989, and since 1991 it has been a constant member of tripartite bodies. Its position on key issues of confrontation have usually been similar to those of trade unions. There are also other organizations, such as the Union of Private Employers, the Union of Free Entrepreneurs and Union "Revival". At the end of 1993 the 13 largest business groups in the country founded a new organization – the Confederation of Bulgarian Industrialists.

Fragmentation of trade union organizations

This process was most evident in Podkrepa after the United Democratic Front (UDF) came to power in 1992 and there was the necessity to formulate a new, purely trade union strategy. The conflict between Podkrepa and "its" government was transferred to within the trade union and caused a split which led to the appearance of new trade union organizations. The first were the National Trade Union (NTU) and the GMCh (geology, metallurgy, chemical) – small organizations that were within the influence of the UDF. Several times in 1992 in conflicts that were crucial for the development of the reform process, NTU and quite often GMCh took positions against CITUB and Podkrepa in their unquestionable support for the government. The split, however, did not remove the source of tension in Podkrepa and a year later a new trade union organization was formed from other splinter groups and individuals, including some that had been expelled from Podkrepa. They formed the Association of Democratic Trade Unions which was also linked to the UDF. The most recent split from Podkrepa was a group from the miners' federation in February 1994. This has formed the National Trade Union Federation – "Miner."

CITUB experienced conflicts at the end of 1990 when it joined the strike that brought down the government. At that time the People's Trade Union "Edinstvo" appeared and declared itself to be a "left alternative" in trade unionism, in line with government policy. Although the CITUB position of non-engagement with any particular political party and keeping trade unionism separate from politics was widely accepted, there were groups, linked to the Bulgarian Socialist Party, that wanted to preserve its influence in the union confederation. It is clear that trade union fragmentation and splits are influenced by shifts and rearrangements among political organizations, or of important groups within them, as well as by attempts by trade unions to conform to certain party policies.

As in Hungary, the question of trade union property became a political issue. The property of CITUB was confiscated by the state in December 1991. Since that time it has been a recurring issue and has played a significant role in the development of inter-union relations and tripartism. Starting from total confrontation between CITUB and Podkrepa on the one hand, and with the government on the other, the issue was coming close to solution in 1993 through the redistribution of assets between the state, CITUB and Podkrepa to a formula of 10:55:35, although CITUB had at least five times more members than Podkrepa. The arrangement could not be executed, however, and because of protests from the other unions, CITUB decided to give up its share in favour of the creation of a fund for additional social security benefits.

Enterprise restructuring and enterprise politics

The 1980s was a period of almost constant change for industrial organizations. The management of the economy, and to some extent the organization of work, were identified as key priorities for economic policy and the development of society. With the evident failure of economic structures to perform adequately, the search for new solutions in redesigning organizations became intensive. Changes were aimed at improving efficiency while shifting the burden of responsibility to enterprise actors and retaining enough central control over the total system. Attempts included the introduction of the brigade form of work organization, worker self-management in enterprises, the transfer of some property rights to the labour collective of enterprises and in 1989, transforming enterprises into "firms", with more managerial autonomy, operating on a "market" basis but within the framework of centrally planned economy (Petkov & Thirkell 1991). Each reform effort, however, did not build upon the achievements of previous reforms but more on the failures. There was no unified integration strategy and they were driven by often contradictory policies. Legislation and mechanisms from different reform periods accumulated, creating increasing sources of contradictory decisions and rising tension. All these affected the situation for reform after 1989.

Embarking on the road to a market economy necessitated new laws and regulations to define the new commercial system, the legal organizational forms of enterprises, and their behaviour. The first steps were made along the lines of the old legislation – through amendments and improvements – while the Commercial Law, the Law for Privatization, the new version of the Labour Code, and other legislative acts were passed. State enterprises faced two choices in the transformation of their legal status: limited company or joint-stock company, both with the state as sole shareholder or stockholder. Although these retain state ownership, there are significant changes. First, the direct link of the state to the ownership of the material assets of the company is abolished. This provides management with considerable autonomy in running their enterprises and gives them greater responsibility for results, with the fate of the organization shifting to them and dependent upon market performance. Secondly, the new entities can set up new enterprises, joint ventures, attract fresh capital and accept new shareholders or stockholders within certain legal limits, which is a major step towards real transformation of state property and privatization. In addition, management and the labour collective, or both, are empowered to apply to the Agency for Privatization for initiating privatization procedures for their enterprises. The major outcome of these changes is that management acquires considerable freedom to formulate new strategies for operating in potentially hostile market environments. In each of our own case studies, new forms of organization were implemented, concentrating on the higher managerial structures but leaving the shop floor organization relatively untouched. Each enterprise had common problems to be addressed:

47

insufficient capital for investment; uncertainties in the newly developing market economy; and management competencies in coping with the pressures of the market. The design of new managerial structures has followed similar lines in all three of the case studies, with Ferromould as the exception, with the emphasis on the decentralized and "flatter" structures. Marketing departments have been introduced to cope with the pressures of the changing economic environment. There has also been the need to reform the accounting process in order to develop financial strategies and manage through financial controls. The reform of personnel departments has been considered to be a lesser priority, although in Bos Air changes were made because of industrial relations within the company. Trade union input in these processes has generally been insignificant. Unions have been informed about the changes but not involved in the development of particular ideas. Their opinions and, through them, the opinions of workers were familiar to management, by using more informal channels and interpersonal connections. Official consultations may take place, but the nature of changes in managerial functions is such that management decides its own strategies and ignores adverse opinion.

The role of middle management in the period of transformation is of increasing importance. The pressure of the process of marketization has set new requirements for products and efficiency, linked to quality and the execution of orders on time. With top management engaged in the search for new strategic solutions, middle managers have acquired an important role in securing the day-to-day operation of enterprises in somewhat chaotic conditions. This devolution of power within managerial levels is best reflected in Startcom where there has been an attempt to create four separate companies along product lines and to differentiate markets and financial results for each of them. In Ferromould this trend is indicated by the intention to introduce profit centres, to make financial results clear and to avoid tensions between the workers and top management. There is also a growing need for industrial discipline to guarantee the quality and the schedule of production. This tendency is reflected at the lowest managerial level and influences relations on the shop floor. In Ferromould this turned out to be a major source of conflict, since the middle managers were mainly Serbians, who the new senior management introduced from a previous venture. But their competence was considered inadequate by the mass of employees and this led to their dismissal. Middle managers also acquire additional powers through their responsibilities for payments, based on collective agreements, and for selecting employees for unpaid leave and redundancy. Directors are also vulnerable from a political point of view. In all four case studies, directors were replaced or dismissed. In three cases – Startcom, Flex Tool and Ferromould – the action against directors had clear political motives and was carried out with key support from the unions. In Bos Air the director was replaced after a strike in 1991, when the old company was split into a number of separate units. Such removals led to the reshuffling of the top levels of management and this enhanced operational autonomy. The middle managers in Ferromould have been somewhat divided in their attitude towards foreigners. They recognize their specialist qualities and the need to work in new ways with strict discipline, but they resent the diminishing status of their own departments. In Startcom the choice of a new general manager rallied the support of political organizations, trade unions and middle management (which provided the channel for the political influence). He, himself, came from a functional department of the company. When it later turned out that he was not the appropriate person for the job, a new post was created – that of executive director. He was also appointed from middle management. Throughout this there is a core of middle management specialists that generates ideas and strategic development. It is not accidental that in the face of privatization the new directors stress that the company cannot be split up and sold in parts. The general manager in Bos Air was appointed from within the company and enjoys almost unlimited power over it. The key role of middle management is to provide him with a protective shield from potential employee opposition to his policies.

Collective bargaining and participation

Collective bargaining is not a new word in the practice of labour relations over the past 50–60 years in Bulgaria. But collective bargaining is still considered to be one of the areas where the changes after 1989 are most expressive and profound, and a guarantee for the democratic transformations in the country. The first evidence for collective agreements as a sporadic event in labour relations in Bulgaria is from the first decade of the century. In 1936 a law on collective bargaining was enacted that made it a comparatively widespread practice. Unfortunately the ideas on which the whole system of industrial relations was based were taken mainly from the corporatist institutions of Italy, and trade unions were well integrated within the Directorate for Labour of the government. Curiously, one of the most successful periods for collective bargaining was in the period between the socialist revolution of 1944 and the nationalization of industrial and bank property in 1948. A unique situation set in, where trade unions enjoyed considerable power and freedom under the new, but still pluralist regime. They had their separate voice in Parliament although strongly influenced and controlled in general by the Communist Party. There was space for real collective bargaining and agreements, especially at branch level with the organizations of employers. After nationalization and the imposition of the Soviet model of industrial relations, collective agreements changed their nature and content thoroughly. The link in industrial relations became the enterprises' interaction with the central authorities. Trade unions were part of the administrative command system, and deprived of the possibility for independent action. Almost all terms and conditions of work were defined in extensive legislation or normative documents, and wages were planned and fixed centrally for the whole country. Collective agreements were restricted to schemes for generating and distributing social benefits through the "social programme" of each enterprise – canteens, specialized or free food, utilization of rest and recreation facilities, sports and cultural events, etc. Trade unions also enjoyed great powers of control and administration over health and safety issues, including stopping work in dangerous enterprises.

Only four months after the political changes of November 1989, the first General Guidelines for Concluding Collective Agreements were adopted by the national tripartite body. By the summer of 1991, along with the General Agreements, there were collective agreements in 37 per cent of the enterprises and a few industry agreements (Thirkell & Tseneva 1992). Collective bargaining became general practice the following year. In 1992 a new and more comprehensive set of guidelines was developed, much more mature and comprehensive, following a Decree on Wages and Collective Bargaining issued by the government in July 1991. The Decree arranged two key issues in an unusual way. Recognition of the trade union organizations in the workplace was secured by a declaration of membership by the corresponding Confederation, which was recognized by the state authorities. The second was the possibility of concluding more than one agreement for the same enterprise (equivalent to the bargaining unit in the West). It was accepted under pressure from Podkrepa, because of their fear that if only the biggest organization at the workplace had negotiating powers – if trade unions could not agree to joint representation (as in the Guidelines 1990) – this would be of definite advantage to CITUB. This model for bargaining was geared to two levels – national and enterprise. In the bargaining round of 1991, 79 per cent of the enterprises concluded agreements and a further 14 per cent were in the process of doing so (Thirkell & Tseneva 1992). However, all these regulations were valid for the enterprises of the state sector and largely insignificant or ignored in the private sector. The case studies indicate that in Flex Tool and Startcom, the two trade union organizations at the plants negotiated together and a single document was produced at the end. They had a joint negotiating team and draft claim, but the content of the claim was discussed and approved separately by the members of each trade union. Participation in the negotiating team was linked to the size of the organization, which meant a dominating position for CITUB. In Bos Air, CITUB and Podkrepa concluded separate agreements. Later, the un-recognized Union of Pilots accepted the agreement of CITUB, and the Union of Engineers and Technical Staff that of Podkrepa. Developments were more interesting in the fourth case – Ferromould, a joint venture with Western capital and management that began operating in 1991. It rented most of its facilities and equipment from a state enterprise that had collapsed on the disintegration of COMECON. At the beginning employees were offered a one-year labour contract. The trade union organization from the previous enterprise decided to intervene and it transpired that the management did not recognize it as being representative. The solution was to organize elections, which legitimated the organization, but the status of the chairman then gave rise to new tension: he had held a similar position in the union organization but was not an employee of the new company. A one-day strike resolved the issue and the chairman was accepted, but this set in motion a strong conflictual element in developing relations with management.

The new Labour Code of 1993 expanded the scope for collective bargaining considerably, especially in terms of payments and conditions of work. It allowed for negotiation on anything that was not determined in laws or other normative documents. The parties were free to negotiate, at national, industrial (or regional) and enterprise levels, all terms and conditions of employment. The key level for bargaining is now the enterprise, where the final sums, and the extent that they can be afforded, are defined. National- and industry-level negotiations are more important for adjusting the macroeconomic parameters of an economy in deep crisis – an "incomes policy" to secure protective minimum or maximum standards – and a statutory minimum wage. At the enterprise level, the parties can agree on improved wages, but at rates no worse than those agreed at national level. The new version of the Labour Code has established a sound basis for the development of industrial relations suitable for the creation of a market economy and a pluralistic democracy in the country. The contextual pressures of a rapidly declining economy, especially of industrial production in the early 1990s, high inflation and shortages tend to produce a somewhat paradoxical situation. In the 1980s, the old regime tried to solve the problems of productivity and efficiency by using as one of its major mechanisms employee motivation through increasing inequalities in earnings. In the period of self-management a coefficient for labour participation was introduced that was decided each month for every worker by the work group – the brigade; that is, wages were linked to results. Trade unions supported this trend. The limits came from communist ideology and from the long tradition of redistributing resources towards loss-making enterprises and levelling of individual earnings in the workplace (Petkov & Thirkell 1991). In the 1990s, the ideology of transformation is soundly based on liberal values, with a reliance upon individual performance. But at the same time "incomes policy" has had to be introduced to control the negative effects of liberalization, the decline of the economy and the recommendations of international financial institutions. In practice, it applies only to state-owned enterprises with the emerging private sector having much more freedom in this respect. The attempt to control wage growth administratively, combined with scarce resources and rapidly falling real incomes, tends to create pressure for income levelling. This can lead to a shift to activities outside the workplace, quite often in the "shadow" economy. Trade union policy is trying to counter this trend by insisting on more sensible links between earnings and economic results in order to promote new patterns of expectations and behaviour, supporting economic and social reforms in the country.

Collective bargaining in the workplace

In the framework procedure, collective agreements are concluded between employers and representative trade unions. The employer is obliged to enter into negotiations within a month, at the latest, after receiving a proposal from the trade union organization, and to provide all necessary information. If the employer breaks the obligation, the company faces the legal requirement of paying a fine. Representative trade unions are the organizations that can produce a certificate of membership of one of the two confederations – CITUB and Podkrepa, which are partners in the national tripartite body. No other trade unions have the right to enter into negotiations when there is a representative trade union in the enterprise. Only one agreement can be made with each employer. The General Assembly of employees elects the organization and the negotiating team. In Startcom and Flex Tool joint representation became a tradition from previous bargaining rounds. At Bos Air, however, five trade union organizations were in existence, three of which were autonomous: those of pilots, of stewardesses and of maintenance technicians and engineers. Management and the representative trade unions from CITUB and Podkrepa accepted that the best solution was for all five to take part in negotiations. This was an informal/official recognition of the power of these occupational groups which was proven later in industrial action. All final agreements have to be in written form, signed and registered in the local labour inspectorate. Changes can be introduced at any time, following mutual agreement of the parties and procedures for negotiating. In case of breach of a collective agreement the employer can be sued in court by the trade union or by individual employees as a party to the contract. Non-organized employees have a choice – to join the collective agreement or to sign an individual labour contract. For joining they have to submit a written application, both to the union committee and to the general manager. All parties in the case study enterprises were involved in collective bargaining in 1991 except for Bos Air, which started in 1992.

In the centralized economic system the Enterprise Wage Fund was subject to strict central control. As Kornai wrote, "hardly any indicator in the [socialist] economy-wide plan is fulfilled more precisely . . . than the target for wages" (Kornai 1980: 377). In Bulgaria, state-owned enterprises have been subject to the Wage Fund Regulations Scheme which is designed to control and regulate the growth of enterprise wage funds and keep them within tight limits. If the limits are exceeded, the enterprise is subject to a higher level of taxation. One the other hand, enterprises that are not state owned are exempt from this regulation and the threat of increased taxes. The case studies show the effects of regulations on collective bargaining. In the three state owned enterprises there was no serious disagreement leading to industrial conflict in the process of collective bargaining. In contrast, at Ferromould conflict over payments and strikes were a constant feature of relations between management and the trade union.

At Flex Tool the process started with management preparing its team and trade unions electing their representatives: four from CITUB and two from Podkrepa. The negotiations were held every Tuesday and Friday and lasted for three weeks. Management played a leading part. Wage bargaining has obviously been the most contentious issue, since, for the first time, wages were to be set through negotiations. The final result has been a so called "pyramid" of wage differentials, with 23 levels for all jobs in the enterprise, excluding the top three managerial levels. The agreement stipulated that in the event of financial problems, the company could reduce wages to the minimum level. The Agreement legitimated the Internal Rules of the Organization of Salaries which allows managers to fix wages over and above the maximum for exceptional performance. The Agreement also covered other terms and conditions such as working time, annual leave, and additional payments. In June 1992, a supplementary agreement was signed for a 55 per cent rise of all wages and salaries. The 1993 round of negotiations followed the requirements of the renewed Labour Code. The trade union team led the negotiations and achieved almost all its objectives. The first issue was to fix the scope of the Agreement in line with the new areas for bargaining opened up by the Labour Code. The Trade Union draft was accepted by management and provided the structure for the bargaining process. The "pyramid" was re-examined and reduced to 14 levels with a minimum salary of 1,740 levs, a maximum of 8,800 levs, and an average of 3,500 levs. This 1993 round of negotiations marked a stage of maturity in collective bargaining and the parties, especially the CITUB affiliates, started to develop internal structures and standards outside the common general prescriptions. In 1993 it was agreed to create a Commission for Administering the Agreement. In the summer of 1993, when the company ran into financial difficulties, trade unions agreed to reschedule payments for inflation compensation so that the bulk (about 60 per cent) would go to the fourth quarter. But the seeds of possible trouble in the future had already been planted. The new General Manager, after a short time, began to demonstrate open annoyance with the presence of trade unions on certain managerial committees and he soon prohibited the accounts department from supplying information to unions. The newly appointed Deputy – the Economic Director – threatened the unions publicly after taking office, and the General Manager privately stated his dreams for a "union-free company".

Developments at Startcom reveal a similar pattern. But a substantial difference was the unchallenged power and leading role of CITUB and the paternalistic style of the enterprise director. Every opportunity was used to supplement salaries in the form of bonuses, compensations and an extremely well-developed social programme offering; cheap food, subsidized holidays, company transport and company apartments. As the former Director put it, "We have preserved everything from socialism and improved some things." When the new General Manager took office a 50 per cent wage increase was announced. The CITUB insisted that the unions be involved so that this did not appear as a managerial gift. Podkrepa also proposed a "fixed sum" pay rise in order to reduce the increases of management. The 1993 round was successful for the unions as a whole, especially in the attempt to counter the negative aspects of the Labour Code, providing advantages for management freedom of action. "The Labour Code of Bulgaria is not valid for Startcom", says the CITUB leader. Friction occurred in the negotiations over lay-offs – and the need for there to be consultation with unions over the criteria applied. The trade unions insisted that years of service should not be the decisive criterion, and stressed the importance of competence and qualification. The agreement secured consultation with the unions on all vital questions, on wage increases and on the mechanism for inflation compensation. Provisions, however, are linked to the economic state of the enterprise since, as the General Manager explained, "There is no guaranteed wage fund any more. There is only money when the company is operating." When, in the summer of 1993, because of market problems, production was cancelled for two months, the trade unions agreed on the rearrangement of work, on lowering payments and even on compulsory leave.

Due to a specific configuration of factors, Bos Air displayed other, peculiar dimensions of the process. The five trade union organizations reached relatively easy agreement on issues of wages, compensation, job protection and the social programme. The basis for wage determination is the national average, which is multiplied by a coefficient for professional categories – commanders, pilots, engineers and technicians. The final differentials resemble those in Western (especially French airlines) which were used as a model. Issues of constant debate are the implementation of health and safety standards, conditions of work, and work schedules. The problems stem from the real value of wages paid and the division between the flying staff and other employees. The flying staff receive payments in hard currency for their periods outside the country. When exchanged for Bulgarian currency this makes wages several times higher than the agreed rate and this heavily distorts the scheme. When the Ministry of Finance ruled that this income should be taxed, pilots threatened industrial action based on health and safety claims. They were backed by the stewardesses but not by other staff.

"Free-riders" are a problem for trade unions in all the cases. The Labour Code permitted non-members to join agreements but it did not specify the mechanism which was left open for local solutions. At Flex Tool and Startcom the non-members could not benefit from the same increases, where the negotiated figures in the collective agreement were higher than in the Labour Code, and management had no right to negotiate higher figures in individual contracts than those shown in the Agreement. The parties agreed that on joining the Agreement non-members should pay a fee equal to 1.2 per cent or 1.1 per cent of annual salary to the enterprise social fund, in practice managed by the unions. The result was that most non-members joined the Agreement and there was even an influx of new members in trade unions. In Bos Air, where the conditions were the same for all employees, trade union membership gave an advantage only in the case of job protection.

Collective bargaining at Ferromould has been characterized by a completely different logic and pattern of action. It started with the signing of a wage agreement and, later, a collective agreement, in June 1992. In fixing wages the different occupational categories have been subject to equalization but the company has proved that this mode of distribution is most beneficial in the difficult situation where new markets had to be gained. At the beginning of 1992 some new demands for higher wages began to be put forward and in March an agreement was reached for wage rises amounting to 25 per cent for March, 30 per cent for April and 40 per cent for May. A one-day strike took place in May 1992 and as a result workers were paid 900 levs each as compensation for January and February. An agreement was reached on the deadline for the conclusion of a collective agreement for 1992 on basic wage bargaining and the system of bonuses, and the payment of inflation rates over and above the increase for April and May. In an additional agreement, the parties agreed to abstain from additional claims for payment and strike action. None the less, the trade union organization declared a strike two months later. The strikers' demands included new wages, compensations for the second quarter, higher allowances for poor working conditions, a bonus system, improved health and safety measures, etc. The arguments for the strike were not easy to accept, managers refused to talk with the strikers and the company filed court proceedings against the participants in the strike. The dispute ended with an agreement to start negotiations on the issues raised, in September 1992. The company agreed not to resort to legal action against the strikers but it insisted on a court ruling concerning the legitimacy of the strike – a move openly directed against the authority of the chairman of the trade union organization. However, the court ruled that the strike was legitimate, which was a heavy blow for management since it was reached with considerable influence from behind the scenes and opened up the possibility for outside interests to exercise influence on the company.

Conclusions

The process of transformation of industrial relations in Bulgaria is already gaining momentum and is developing at all levels of the industrial relations system. The inherited centralized model characteristic of the planned economy is being modified into an emerging system which has a number of fundamentally new elements, although there are remnants of the old values such as egalitarian expectations in relation to the distribution process. One of these is the tripartite structure for social partnership and co-ordination of interests, tested in 1991–2 and functioning fully since the beginning of 1993. However, the operation of tripartism is conditioned by the economic environment, and the content of national negotiations are directly dependent on the development of economic reforms and political changes. A "triangle" incorporating industrial relations, economic reform and political changes influences both the limitations of tripartism and its potential for development. When reforms are advancing – as in the first half of 1991 and in 1992 –

industrial relations undergo dynamic changes as space is created for the formulation of new strategies. Such strategies at the national level produced a temporary consensus between social partners during the period of shock therapy and macroeconomic stabilization in 1991. Confrontational strategies developed in 1992 by the government and the unions, which led to destabilization of the economy, blocked the development of industrial relations and generated tensions in the political system. In general, the dynamics of industrial relations at the national and branch levels in Bulgaria are highly variable and uncertain and are not characterized by continuity. Even the introduction of legal regulation and the institutionalization of industrial relations does not lead to a more consistent and stable direction of change.

At the national level, trade unions operate as a key partner with clearly defined, though not always successful, strategies. At enterprise level their activity varies and is more complicated. In two of our case studies there have been periods of militant pluralism and spontaneous actions. The employers and trade unions are far more successful in "processing" problems and conflicts through the regulatory mechanisms laid down by the new Labour Code and the Law for Collective Labour Disputes. It is also true that in a number of cases management, especially the directors, channel the energy of unions towards the central agencies, attempting to use them as an instrument to press for solutions to company problems, such as access to credit, and greater autonomy. In conditions of uncertainty, trade unions retain a surprisingly high membership, even in declining enterprises and branches. Their power is derived from developed national, branch and workplace structures, as well as from the ability to represent interests and to be an effective voice of worker interests.

Management is undergoing the slowest and least visible transformation. On the one hand, middle management as individuals rather than as a distinct group, try to use the period of transformation to obtain greater autonomy and to develop new competences in such functional areas as business and market strategy, design, control, and financial information. On the other hand, senior management is emerging from a crisis of instability – caused by the massive replacement of directors for political and other non-business reasons – and is gradually becoming one of the most influential groups in the transition to a market economy. The empirical evidence for this new, independent role is to be found especially in their privatization initiatives as well as in developing major trade and investment policies freed from bureaucratic control.

Despite three years' experience, collective bargaining in enterprises is more like a "dry run" than a real process of regulation and co-ordination of principally contradictory interests. The scope for negotiation is highly limited. Control over wages is implemented at national, branch and workplace level according to the recommendations of the IMF. In these conditions negotiations function as a mechanism for the distribution of predetermined, limited resources. Attempts by unions and employers to compensate for the inadequacy of the Wage Fund by supplementary payments and fringe benefits do not produce significant results. In this way collective agreements do not fix relative gains for each of the parties but are more a demonstration that the partners agree to minimize their respective losses. The main objective is not to exceed the limit that would threaten the enterprise with bankruptcy.

If it is necessary to define the distinctive feature of the Bulgarian transition in terms of industrial relations, it probably starts with the "illogical" economic reforms which started in 1991 with "shock therapy", but with the initial success fading away within 6 months. In 1992 the structural reforms started, not with the privatization of state enterprises but with restitution of town properties and land, which produced a boom for the small private sector in trade and services. State industrial enterprises were trapped in a process of gradual financial decline. In this situation the formal, centrally regulated economic reform is just one type of transformation that determines industrial relations. The second, almost invisible layer of changes in the economy, with its roots in the "socialist" private sector and the preserved resources of the ruling communist elite, is also an important factor shaping the dynamics of industrial relations, although not necessarily in a positive direction. How this counterposing of the "formal" and "informal" layers of industrial relations will develop, and how regulated versus non-regulated changes will interrelate and have real structural and institutional outcomes in Bulgaria remains open to question.

CHAPTER 3

The Czech and Slovak Republics

Ludovit Cziria

Both the Czech and Slovak republics are now undergoing a process of social transformation. In November 1989, at the time of the collapse of the communist regime, the Czechoslovakian economy was in a comparatively good position. It had a low foreign debt and low inflation, with a well-developed industrial tradition and a skilled labour force. Strategies for economic transformation have proceeded hand in hand with political changes. The first free elections were held in June 1990 and the implementation of economic reforms began in early 1991. These consisted of: the liberalization of domestic prices; the liberalization of foreign trade; establishing a convertible currency; devaluation of the *koruna* (crown); restitution of property; privatization of small busi-nesses; and deregulation of the labour market. These measures have created the basis for the transition to a market economy.

The privatization process

The privatization of small-scale enterprises in trade, service and manufacturing, but excluding agriculture, was carried out in two stages. In the first, only Czechoslovak citizens were allowed to participate, while in the second, foreigners could also purchase businesses. The process was controlled by the Ministry for the Administration of National Property and Privatization (MSNMP). During 1991 more than 30,000 business units were converted into private ownership.

The privatization of large-scale state enterprises began in 1992 and allowed for the setting up of joint-stock companies, investment companies and co-operatives. In preparation for privatization, state owned enterprises were transformed into state-owned joint-stock companies. The Privatization Act allowed for various forms of change in ownership, including: the restitution to former owners of property nationalized after 1948; direct sale to vendors; the establishment of joint ventures with foreign firms; and privatization through the public distribution of vouchers which citizens could use to purchase shares. In contrast to the privatization of small firms, in this case foreign nationals were allowed to participate.

State owned enterprises were divided into two categories for the purposes of privatization. The first consists of those which will not be privatized in the short term: for example, power plants, telecommunications, railways, etc. The second, enterprises in manufacturing industry which are the subject of the present Programme A. The privatization of these enterprises was organized in two stages – 2,300 at first, followed by a second stage of 1,800. In the first of these, which started in late 1991, vouchers were the principal method of privatization, being offered to the general public aged over 18 years. These were bought by 5.95 million people in the Czech republic and by 2.6 million in the Slovak republic. Each voucher contained investment tokens to the value of Kčs 1,000. In this wave, investment privatization funds (IPF) have played a key role. There were 429 of these, 264 of them in the Czech republic and 165 in the Slovak republic. The total assets invested in the first stage of privatization amounted to 300 billion Kčs, corresponding to 300 million shares each with a nominal value of Kčs 1,000. Of these, the Czech National Property Fund (FNM) purchased 206.4 million shares in 943 state owned joint stock companies, the Slovak FNM 90.1 million shares in 487 joint-stock companies and the Federal FNM 2,857 shares in 61 joint-stock companies.

A consequence of the first wave of privatization was that investment funds own about 63 per cent of the 278 million shares offered for sale, that is, about two-thirds of the shares of privatized enterprises. Thus the original aim of creating a broad stratum of individual shareholders – popular capitalism – has been achieved to only a limited extent. In most enterprises the majority of shares are held by investment trusts and within these, shares are concentrated in a small number of funds. Two per cent of these trusts own approximately half of all the shares sold.

Therefore there is a high degree of share concentration – an unexpected result of the privatization, in which the potential role of investment funds was underestimated. This raises a question about how these funds will exercise their control over enterprises, and also about their relationship with individual shareholders. So far, the voucher method of privatization has not yielded large financial assets, sufficient for restructuring industry, for modernization or for the purchase of technical know-how. To date, privatization has consisted of the transformation of state owned enterprises into joint-stock companies, in the creation of more than 2.5 million individual shareholders, and the beginnings of a stock market.

In the first half of 1993, individual shareholders received their shares. In spite of some initial problems following the partition of Czechoslovakia into two independent states, in both republics the shares were also allocated to the citizens of the other republic. During the second half of 1993 the second wave of privatization began in the Czech republic. Compared with the first, more authority was given to the MSNMP to make decisions on the method of privatization and to evaluate the privatization proposals of enterprises. In the Slovak republic, the second stage was planned to begin in the second half of 1994. It is expected that the use of vouchers will be reduced and more emphasis will be given to direct sales and joint ventures. This general picture of privatization can be illustrated by our various case studies (see Table 3.1).

The case studies indicate how different types of ownership change influenced enterprise restructuring and labour relations. In the case of Slovcar, privatization was implemented by the decentralization of the former state owned joint-stock company into several independent enterprises and relatively independent operating plants. The company was privatized by a German company which purchased 80 per cent of the equity with the remaining 20 per cent of shares held by the state.

Table 3.1 Czech and Slovak enterprises: a profile of three case study enterprises.

Enterprise	SPRINGS	SLOVCAR	FLOORPLAST
Branch	Mechanical springs	Car manufacture	Plastic products
Number of employees	1990: 2,012 1991: 1,400	1990: 4,609 1992: 2,788	1990: 2,452 1993: 1,700
Legal status	Privatized by voucher method (1st wave of privatization)	Privatized, foreign ownership	Joint-stock company (2nd wave of privatization)

According to the negotiated deal, the German company will increase its stake gradually to 97 per cent. In the Springs joint-stock company, privatization was undertaken through the voucher method. This allocated 48 per cent of shares to citizens, 40 per cent to employees, 9 per cent for direct sale to interested foreign buyers, and the remaining 3 per cent reserved for restitution. In practice, the outcome has been a management buy-out, with 24 members of top management owning a total of 40 per cent of the shares. Some joint ventures have been established with foreign companies. Floorplast is included in the second wave of privatization to be carried out in 1994. This joint-stock company will be divided into three independent entities, with Floorplast and Tefolan to be privatized through the voucher method and a separate machinery plant to be offered for direct sale.

Privatization and enterprise strategy

In the former command economy, the strategies of VHJs (units of production and economy) and those of the enterprise were formulated by branch ministries. The enterprise merely implemented plans (5-year and 1-year) reflecting the strategies of higher management. In the command economy, production and development strategies were derived from the state plan for each industrial branch, with plans handed down to the VHJ, and from the VHJ to the enterprise. Figure 3.1 illustrates this mechanism.

National economic strategy directed 60 to 70 per cent of Czech and Slovak foreign trade to COMECON countries. Enterprise had no

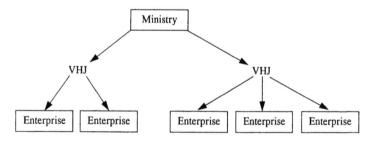

Figure 3.1 The place of the enterprises in strategy formation.

independence, their only aim being to fulfil, or over-fulfil, the plan; they had no interest in generating higher profits because these were handed over to the state. The state distributed funds centrally through the ministries to the VHJs and these then allocated them to the enterprises. This regime did not require rational action by enterprises, nor efficient performance; on the contrary, in many enterprises inefficient production was subsidized. Moreover, the conduct of foreign trade was centralized through a specialist ministry and particular business organizations, usually belonging to the VHJs. Enterprises had no access to hard currency nor (with a few exceptions) to international trade. Enterprises had no legal rights and their autonomy in formulating strategy was limited by legislation – a situation which inhibited enterprise initiative, making the enterprise rigid and inflexible. This led to stagnation and a decline in economic growth in the late 1980s. As a result, the leadership of the Communist Party decided in 1987 to implement a more flexible and more effective economic strategy based on the liberalization of central planning, an increase in foreign trade with Western countries, and more autonomy for state owned enterprises. These provisions were set out in the *Principles for the rearrangement of economic mechanisms* (1988). The main intention was to reduce central control over enterprises, to increase the role of market mechanisms – prices, costs, profits, etc. – and to give enterprises legal independence. In this new strategy, the restructuring of organizations was a major priority, with the aim of breaking down the large VHJs, with their hierarchical, and inflexible structures and top-heavy administrations. The largest VHJ had over 70,000 employees, and the average was 20,000 employees. The constituent enterprises belonging to VHJs were also very large: for example, the enterprises controlled by the federal government had, on average, 4,800 employees, and those controlled by the Czech or Slovak governments an average of 2,400 employees. In 1988–9 the VHJs were abolished and a total of 2,278 state owned enterprises were created (43 per cent of them by local authorities). However, the transformation of VHJs led to the emergence of new giant enterprises; for example, under the Federal Ministry of Metallurgy, Machines and Electro-industry, 89 state owned enterprises were founded, with an average number of 7,800 employees. Indeed, a third of the newly created state owned enterprises had an average of 20,000 employees. Accordingly, the strategy of establishing smaller, more flexible, enterprises was not achieved.

In reality, radical changes in economic strategy began to affect the behaviour of the enterprises from 1991, based on preparations in 1990 when two new acts were passed: The (Renewed) State Owned Enterprise Act and the Joint-Stock Company Act. These provided the legal basis for enterprises to operate in both domestic and foreign markets, as well as for privatization to be pursued. Enterprises were exposed to market forces including foreign competition. In order to liberalize foreign trade, the domestic convertibility of the Kčs was introduced and the monopoly of the foreign trading companies was weakened. Fewer state subsidies were given to loss-making enterprises, which were compelled to work more efficiently and to develop and to implement their own business strategies. There was a radical change in the orientation of foreign trade because of the political changes affecting COMECON countries and, in particular, the disintegration of the market in the former Soviet Union; trade with Western countries increased considerably.

During 1991 and the first half of 1992, the strategies of many the enterprises was aimed at minimizing decreases in production and entering new markets. During the second half of 1992 and in 1993 enterprises focused their strategy on survival; the situation of the Slovak enterprises was worsened by the partition of Czechoslovakia into two states. The formation of enterprise strategies for survival was constrained by two facts: their high debts and their lack of funds for investment. This applied especially to manufacturing and engineering companies, and an important part of their policy was to identify new markets and to modernize their technology. Often the quickest way was to co-operate with foreign partners and set up joint ventures.

For Springs, the business strategy was focused on the diversification of production, the modernization of the production programme, the formation of a marketing function, and finding new markets in the West. To improve the efficiency of operations, the strategy of the enterprise was based on decentralization and the establishment of smaller, independent units. For this purpose, the trade company GB-Trading was founded and joint ventures established. The whole enterprise was reorganized into semi-autonomous divisions which were later transformed into independent enterprises within the framework of an overall holding company.

At Slovcar, a new limited company was established. Business strategy was orientated towards new markets in central Europe and based upon the technical know-how of its German parent company. The enterprise was restructured into independent organizational units based on the German two-tier management system. At the same time, many parts of production are subcontracted to external suppliers. In Floorplast a new business strategy was introduced, signifying a change in orientation from the markets of the former COMECON countries to those of Western economies. It introduced new products and technologies and restructured its operations on a divisional basis.

Organizational restructuring and the role of middle management

The organization structures of Czech and Slovak enterprises under the old regime were shaped by the economic system in which they operated. They were not required to carry out entrepreneurial activities, but only to fulfil the plan. They were allowed to produce inefficiently and they could not go bankrupt. There was a national job evaluation system and workers were paid by a tariff system valid for the whole country; this promoted the levelling of wages and salaries and there was no incentive to intensify outputs. Managers were not interested in reducing the number of jobs: on the contrary, they tried to have as many employees as possible. This had advantages for them; larger enterprises meant higher salaries while reserves of labour facilitated the fulfilment of plans and offered a more flexible response to problems caused by delays in the delivery of raw materials.

These enterprises had multi-level pyramid structures with top-heavy and inefficient management systems. Most of the social facilities – culture and recreation centres, kindergartens and crèches, canteens, etc. – belonged to them. Standardized organization structures were imposed by the VHJs upon enterprises and they could not reorganize without the consent of the VHJs' general management. An important innovation affecting the internal structure of enterprises – and forms of participation by workers in management – was the introduction of the brigade system of work in 1985. Between then and 1989 this working system became widespread; in 1987, 18,000 labour collectives were organized in this way, with a total of 500,000 members in the Czech and Slovak republics, representing about 12 per cent of all production workers in the more important industrial branches. This form of organization, consisting of relatively autonomous work teams (brigades), decided issues of internal labour organization, the division of labour, the utilization of resources, and the payment of brigade members. Brigades had many features in common with the autonomous or semi-autonomous groups operating in Western countries, particularly in Scandinavia. Although the brigade system was initiated and supported by the Communist Party, it had good results, with an increase in the level of participation of workers who were interested in contributing to the solution of problems. There were increases in labour productivity and this form of work organization facilitated the elimination of uniform remuneration levels and the introduction of higher earnings for more efficient workers. It was this which most motivated workers to transfer to this work system (Cziria 1992). When political pressure for the implementation of brigades ended in 1989, this form of work organization lost its special features and its attraction. In some cases, brigade organization withered away, but in enterprises where teams performed well, they were integrated into the changing organizational structures of the enterprises.

In the transition to market conditions since 1991, enterprises have begun to experience pressures for efficiency. This has also been felt by enterprises that are not yet privatized, such as Floorplast. Changes in organization structure have operated in two main directions. One is the slimming down of enterprises, starting with the divestment of those units not directly needed for production, such as those concerned with the social facilities: for example, kindergartens and crèches have been handed over to local authorities, while others, such as cultural centres, canteens, and recreation and training centres, are often leased to private operators. For example, Springs has dismissed its security guards and hired a private firm to carry out this service. Springs also disposed of its cars and now leases vehicles from private firms. In some cases, the manufacture of parts is subcontracted out. The other main direction for the implementation of changes to the structures of enterprises is the process of divisionalization. This has brought about radical changes to the traditional structures of enterprises. Some functional departments – engineering, manufacture, finance, personnel – have been disbanded and more semi-autonomous divisions with responsibility for financial results in the form of cost or profit centres set up. These changes have affected the role of both top and middle management, with senior managers now able to direct their attention to enterprise strategy. After the transition to the divisional organization, the attention of the top management is freed for the development of enterprise strategy.

In Slovcar the management comprises three levels: senior managers

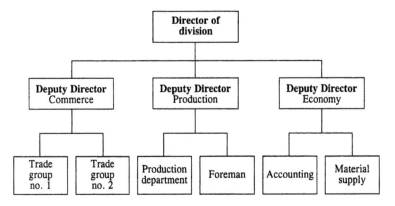

Figure 3.2 Organizational structure of Slovcar.

consist of heads of plants and departments and have strategic responsibilities; middle managers are those who are responsible for implementing strategic plans at the operational level; and junior managers
have day-to-day operational targets to achieve. The organizational chart
is shown in Figure 3.2.

Middle managers are now responsible for financial results and, as
divisional heads, they are involved in strategy formulation processes.
They now have to use resources more effectively, and as a result
they have had to develop new competences through attending some management development programmes. Some have been unable to acquire
these new skills and as a result they have been redeployed. After privatization, some enterprises, including Springs, set up holding company
structures, within which divisions have gained legal status and operate as
independent business entities. This has reinforced the need for both senior and middle managers to develop new strategic and operational skills.
The general trend of organizational restructuring – as witnessed in our
case studies – is towards divisionalization. Traditional pyramid structures have been transformed into product-oriented, semi-autonomous
divisions, operating either as cost or as profit centres. In Springs, an
interesting development was the setting up of a corporate treasury. This
monitors the performance of the different divisions and operating units,
and offers loans and funds for various ventures.

Trade union responses

Under the former regime, trade unions functioned as transmission belts for the economic plans of the Communist Party. They were instrumental in obtaining employee compliance and loyalty to the regime. The main mechanisms for achieving this were low cost recreation facilities and other fringe benefits on the one hand, and care for social and working conditions on the other. After the collapse of the former regime, trade unions lost their original functions. It was not accidental that directly after the events of November 1989, thousands of independent strike committees were established which organized the general strike of 27 November 1989 that demanded the abolition of the official trade union. At the Trade Union Congress in March 1990 the delegates decided to dissolve this union and, at the same time, approved a newly established General Congress of Trade Unions formed on ILO principles. In January 1990 the independent Slovak Trade Union was formed, and transformed itself within a month into the Trade Union Confederation of the Slovak republic. A similar development took place in the Czech republic, and in March 1990 both national confederations established the Czech and Slovak Trade Union Confederation (CSKOZ). It is notable that even within the federal state, the trade unions agreed from the beginning on the principle of confederation in the spirit of various international engagements and agreements on trade union activities. CSKOZ had about 6 million members – compared with 7.5 million members in the former communist-controlled confederation, and consisted of 21 federal, 20 Czech and 22 Slovak trade unions. Only one organization, the Trade Union Confederation of Art and Culture, with about 100,000 members, operated outside the CSKOZ. Overall membership of trade unions remains high, at about 80 per cent. The principles of the newly-formed confederation were: autonomy, voluntarism and independence; protection of employees' rights; and securing trade union rights by legal means.

From April 1990 until the end of 1992 CSKOZ had the structure shown in Figure 3.3. Arising from the partition of Czechoslovakia, the Czech and Slovak Trade Union Confederation (CSKOZ) terminated its activities on 20 November 1993 when both national unions joined the International Confederation of Free Trade Unions. At the time of writing, some foreign relations are co-ordinated jointly, but other co-operative activities are limited to the exchange of information in the spirit of trade

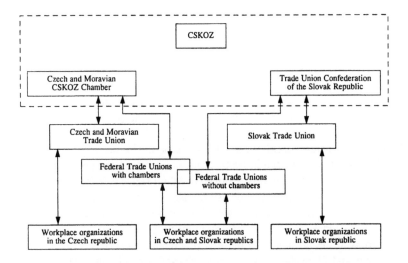

Figure 3.3 Organizational structure of Czech and Slovak trade unions.

union solidarity. In the Slovak republic there has been some decline in membership as a result of a number of factors. These include the reorientation of trade unionism from distributing benefits to compliant members to that of defending the basic rights of workers; the changing composition of the workforce caused by the recession and by structural changes in the economy, and the formation of new trade associations or quasi-trade unions, often lacking a regular organization structure as, for example, the "Workers' Forum", the "Teachers' Forum", etc., and also of such other trade unions as the Independent Christian Trade Union of Slovakia. Trade union membership has now stabilized in Slovakia: in 1993 there were about 1.8 million members, compared with 2.4 million members of the former communist-led confederation. The Slovakian Confederation of Trade Unions has 46 member unions of various sizes; the ten largest have 1,325,000 registered members, which represents 74 per cent of all trade unionists (1993). In the process of the economic transformation, trade unions are crucial in representing workers' interests and the main functions of the Slovakian Trade Union Confederation are: to protect the basic social security of workers, adolescents, women, pensioners and families; to negotiate wages; to maintain workers' democratic rights; and to protect working and living conditions and the environment.

Despite demands for radical action, trade unions prefer the path of co-operation, especially with the government. At the same time, highly contentious problems have to be resolved, derived from the implementation of economic and social reforms such as dealing with unemployment, rising prices, stagnation of wages, and reduced social benefits. Currently the most important goal of both government and trade unions is to maintain social peace. This continues to be successful despite rising tensions. In spite of the successful activities of trade unions at the national level, their legal position in enterprises has weakened. This occurred when the Labour Code was revised in 1990. Trade unions' former right to prevent the dismissal of workers was removed and their rights to information and to participation in enterprise decision-making were limited. Changes in the position of trade unions are well illustrated by the fact that in the past they were represented automatically in meetings of senior management, whereas at the present time there is practically no access to them. At Springs and Floorplast new unions were established by the transformation of the former organizations. In Slovcar there was a different process in the formation of the union organization. In 1991, when the company was formed, no trade union existed, but later, management created a Workers' Plant Council (based on the German model). Since this form of worker participation was not recognized either in the Czechoslovak labour code or in other relevant labour relations acts, management decided after a short period to support the establishment of a trade union organization. This now co-operates with management in improving working conditions and wages.

Collective bargaining and participation

In conjunction with the changing role of trade unionism, the functions of collective bargaining and of collective agreements have altered. In the old system – where it was the partner of enterprise management – the trade union's role was to support management and to mobilize workers to fulfil the aims of the plan. This affected the nature of collective bargaining, which was largely a formal process where there was no bargaining over conflicting interests. Collective agreements contained many formal provisions associated with the relationship between management and the trade union committee about such matters as labour and recreation. From a practical point of view, more important were those parts of the collective agreement which dealt with financial matters, such as bonus systems and the use of funds for cultural and social needs. These funds were based on the obligation to allocate to them 2 per cent of the total enterprise wage bill. Neither collective bargaining nor collective agreements dealt with issues of job security, since there were no large-scale redundancies. In these conditions collective labour relations were highly formal and determined solely by management. The participation of workers in enterprise decision-making was also highly formal and was realized only through trade union representatives. In the field of industrial relations an important event, under the former regime, was the State Enterprise Act of 1988 which provided for the creation of participatory bodies in enterprises. These were elected by employees through workers' councils, workers' assemblies, and delegates of brigades. These forums – alongside trade unions – enabled worker participation in the internal organization and management of enterprises. During their period of operation – of roughly one and a half years – they took part in the elections of directors so that for the first time in the history of the socialist state a greater number of managers were appointed who were not members of the Communist Party. At the same time, more autonomy was created for development of workers' participation in enterprise decision-making (Cziria 1990).

This was the position in Czech and Slovak enterprises in November 1989. With the transition to market mechanisms in the economy, labour relations in enterprises changed gradually; as management became obliged to apply unpopular measures such as the dismissal of workers, control of wages, and tighter labour discipline, so the role of trade unionism and collective bargaining changed as differences in the interests of management and employees became more noticeable. In 1990 participatory bodies in enterprises were dismantled, such as workers' councils and workers' assemblies. A revised State Owned Enterprise Act abolished the election of general managers, and later a new Joint-Stock Company Act introduced new institutional forums such as general assemblies of shareholders, and boards of directors. The national-level General Agreements of 1991–4 shaped the nature of collective bargaining at branch level, which in turn provided the context for agreements at enterprise level. Generally, these covered all employees (whether or not they were trade union members) except top managers, who left trade unions to join a newly-formed Association of Managers.

In most enterprises – including the three case studies – forms of regular communication between management and representatives of the trade union, together with the appropriate procedures, have been set up. However, issues of discussion do not include management strategy, nor questions of restructuring. In joint-stock companies, matters of corporate performance have been transferred to shareholders' meetings, while employees are informed at trade union meetings. At Floorplast all employees and the trade union organization are kept informed about issues of company strategy.

Collective bargaining is potentially conflictual because it includes questions of employment, job security, safety and health, hours of work, wages, and forms of co-operation between management and trade unions. An important event for the development of collective bargaining occurred in late 1992, when the government abolished state control over the regulation of wages so that these could be related to the economic conditions of enterprises. Overall, processes of collective bargaining can be characterized as being consensual rather than conflictual, since both parties make every attempt to understand the possible limits for compromise. According to the law, trade unions are entitled to strike and the employers to apply a lock-out policy when there is no agreement, although strikes are not permitted to enforce rights set out in the collective agreement. Such disputes must be resolved by conciliation, mediation or arbitration. The general situation in collective bargaining is demonstrated by the fact that from 1990 until the first half of 1994 no general or very important strikes have occurred. The strikes that have taken place have been of a "threat" nature and lasted only a few hours. Detailed cross-sectional studies on small privately-owned enterprises are not available, although it seems that trade union organizations do not exist in most of these. There is no collective negotiation on working conditions and wages, and no collective agreements are concluded. In return for their higher wages and salaries, employees often accept inferior working conditions. Analysis of the Springs, Slovcar and Floorplast case studies suggest that wages, employees' safety and health and the protection of their rights are all the subject of collective bargaining and are included in the Collective Agreement. Comparing the present collective bargaining agreements with those under the former regime, at the time of writing there is an emphasis upon employment conditions and wages, while previously the emphasis was upon recreation, culture and sport. The trade union structures in our case studies correspond more or less to the enterprise structures. In Springs there is trade union organization within the divisions, with most of the bargaining competences delegated to this level. At the enterprise level the trade union committee is composed of the chairs of the various workshop committees.

Tripartism/corporatism

For the development of collective labour relations, an important event was the creation of tripartite institutions incorporating representatives of the government, trade unions and employers. Three tripartite Councils of Economic and Social Agreement (RHSD) were established. A federal council was established on 3 October 1990 and national councils on 10 October 1990. The most important function of the RHSD is to discuss the government's proposals affecting employment conditions, social policy and the living standards of the population before they are submitted to Parliament. The main object of tripartism is to create conditions for economic transformation and for social reform by achieving consensus and maintaining social peace. The first subjects of tripartite negotiations were amendments to the Labour Code and the drafts of the Employment Act and Collective Bargaining Act. Another very important topic was the determination of the minimum wage. In relation to the Labour Code, the issue of the rights of trade unions to participate in the decision-making processes of enterprises was very contentious. Despite a strike threat by the trade unions, Parliament approved the limitation of trade union rights in enterprises and the increased the authority of management. The first concrete result of tripartite discussion was the signing of the Federal Agreement and the two National General Agreements for 1991 in Bratislava on 28 January 1991. In these Agreements the emphasis - besides a minimum wage - was on the regulation of wages according to the economic performance of enterprises and on the index-ation of earnings in relation to price rises. This agreement contributed to a comparatively low wage inflation - about 16 per cent in 1991 - compared to price inflation of about 59 per cent. Thus, *real* wages decreased by about 26 per cent in 1991.

The General Agreements for 1991, 1992 and 1993 played an important role in collective bargaining at the level of industrial branches. However, these were not legally binding but instead consisted of the agreement of the social partners, with their voluntary commitment to abide by its provisions. In 1991, the most important issue was determining a monthly minimum wage of Kčs 2,000 – compared with the national average of Kčs 3,500. This led to an increase in the wage bills of enterprises, causing a growth in the general level of unemployment, which reached 4 per cent in 1991 in the Czech republic and 12 per cent in the Slovak republic. In 1992, the main issue was the abolition of the regulation of wages – which was realized in October 1992. The general problem for both tripartism and the 1992 General Agreement is the question of the legal enforcement of agreements made in the tripartite forums. Trade unions argue for the legal validity of all the provisions of tripartite agreements. With the partition of Czechoslovakia, federal tripartism was terminated by the two national RHSDs of the Czech republic and the Slovak republic operating independently. Former decisions on labour relations – until 1994 – remain valid in both republics. The national RHSDs continue to operate according to the original structure; in the Slovak republic the RHSD consists of representatives from the government, the association of employers, and trade unions. The RHSDs have boards of directors, chairmen and vice-chairmen, the secretary-generals; and administrations. The chairmen are representatives of the government, one vice-chairman represents trade unions, and the other, employers. The negotiations of the national RHSDs results in agreements, opinions and recommendations. The results of negotiations are binding on the participants, once all three parties have given their consent. In the Slovak republic, the most serious questions in the tripartite discussions have been the preparation of the 1993 national budget, fiscal policy, social policy and policy for prices. The General Agreement for 1994 has the following sections: general provisions; general duties of the partners; interests of trade unions and of employees; ratification of the European Social Charter and ILO Conventions; economic policy – principles and obligations of government; labour earnings policy – principles and obligations of the parties; and social policy – obligations of the government. On the whole, it can be argued that tripartism has played a positive role since 1991 in maintaining social peace in Czechoslovakia, and later in the Czech and Slovak republics.

Interest articulation

As a result of the transition to a market economy, a certain differentiation of employees' interests, and of their manifestation, can be observed in enterprises. In the previous system, senior management, trade unions and the local organizations of the Communist Party shared a common interest to fulfil the plan because their bonuses, careers and social position depended on it. Workers had their job grades and wages determined by the national tariff, and remuneration for fulfilling the plan was not sufficiently motivating. The situation is now entirely different and new group interests are forming. Some general indications of change include the fact that management, and in particular senior management, dominates enterprise decision-making and has the responsibility for economic results. This, together with their higher salaries, differentiates managers from other employees. In some cases, management has participated in privatization through management buy-outs, which has strengthened their position as managers and as owners of blocks of enterprise shares, and they are beginning to behave as proprietors. Today, managers are no longer members of trade unions and they pursue their interests through professional associations. Management and trade unions are partners in collective bargaining, often articulating antagonistic interests over such areas as wages, social security and working conditions. In enterprises with a majority of ownership in the hands of foreign capital, the dominant position of the management in decision-making is even stronger, and there are isolated cases where management has tried to make agreements on working conditions without bargaining with trade unions.

So far, we can make few generalizations on the articulation of the interests of middle managers or of other groups of workers. The strongest force for the differentiation of interests is in the participation in the privatization of enterprises. Within the framework of the second stage of privatization in the Slovak republic, the discussion has focused upon employee shares. There exists a tendency for certain groups of managers to obtain as much property as possible through privatization. This aim shapes their activities, both within and outside enterprises. After the deregulation of wages, it can often happen that managers secure higher salaries, even when their enterprises are not profitable. In both state owned enterprises and in joint ventures, the articulation of employees' interests is also realized through their representation on supervisory boards where employees elect half of the members in state owned enterprises and a third in the joint venture companies.

Supervisory boards in state owned enterprises express opinions on the economy, corporate development, the use of profits, and the appointment of general managers. The analyses of the three case studies, Springs, Slovcar and Floorplast demonstrate that in these enterprises trade unions are the main representative institutions for the articulation of employee interests in their relations with management. In privatized enterprises such as Springs, a general assembly of shareholders exists and because many employees are shareholders, their interests can be expressed through this forum, though with little influence.

Conclusions

The political changes in the former Czechoslovakia after November 1989 also enabled various changes in the economic and social spheres. The basic elements of the transition to a market economy have been: the liberalization of domestic prices and foreign trade; the internal convertibility of the currency; the liberalization of the labour market; and privatization. These changes have provided a new environment for enterprise activities and labour relations, particularly the establishment of conditions for the reform of trade unions as independent, voluntary organizations representing the interests of employees. To understand the impact of these changes for the operation of enterprises it is important to bear in mind that organizational restructuring had already started before November 1989. During 1988-9 the so-called Economic Production Units (VHJ) had been abolished, having been, in the command economy, the key link in the top-down management between ministries and enterprises. Although this experiment of restructuring and decentralization of the very large enterprises failed, it nevertheless yielded an important result: the enterprises gained more independence in decision-making. When they started operating in the market environment in 1991, they were able to implement their own strategies in production, trade and management. The most important task for enterprises was to find new markets for their products, mainly in market economy countries. This required not only strategic independence but also the ability to operate efficiently. Because of those demands, together with the ending of state subsidies for ineffective enterprises, the restructuring of enterprises continued. This process started well before privatization, so that enterprise restructuring was initiated more by the introduction of market forces than by changes in property relations.

More than 8.5 million citizens participated in the privatization process, but only 2.5 million of them were direct shareholders of enterprise shares (as at 1993). The remainder have put their vouchers into Privatization Investment Funds (IPF) which have bought the majority of enterprise shares. Ten of the IPFs – about 2 per cent of all of them – are owners of about 50 per cent of all shares sold. This concentration of property is continuing as individual shareholders sell their shares to them. The state also continues to own a considerable percentage of shares even after privatization.

Independent trade union organizations have been formed in enterprises, and at the branch level these organizations are integrated into the Trade Union Confederation. Trade unions base their activities on the protection of the interests and rights of employees against those of employers. At the same time, the government has accepted the role of trade unions in tripartite bargaining about all fundamental changes emerging from social and economic transformation. Even so, the govern-ment has enforced changes in legislation which has weakened their former position. They now have less influence in the dismissal of employees, the remuneration of employees, and in the activities of the social funds. Through the abolition of workers' councils, the participation of employees has been weakened in enterprise decision-making and collective bargaining is the major mechanism of labour relations. In the tripartite RHSDs, General Agreements are concluded between the government, trade unions and employers for each year. Although these agreements have no legal standing, they provide a framework for collective bargaining and for collective agreements at branch levels. Conflicts in labour relations are caused by various circumstances such as, for instance, little experience in negotiation, the extreme positions of representatives of both trade unions and management and the aim to bring "politics" into labour relations.

Growing pressure for efficient performance has led enterprise managers to reorganize company structures. The traditional pyramid forms of organization have been replaced by the establishment of divisional structures. Enterprises have ceased to operate as social units and now subcontract many of their former activities. Organizational restructuring has led to an increase in unemployment but up to 1994 social peace has

79

been preserved in both the Czech and Slovak republics. This has been helped by the co-ordinated policies of the trade unions, which in enterprises generally operate on a single union basis. However, there have been no extensive bankruptcies and labour relations may become more bitter if there is massive dismissal of workers. The government, employers and trade unions are well aware of this risk, and the analysis of the case studies shows that changes in labour relations are determined mainly by market mechanisms, by the liberalization of labour markets, and by changes in labour legislation. In the longer term, privatization and how this affects the nature of both management and trade unions is likely to have a major impact upon labour relations.

CHAPTER 4

Hungary

Làjos Héthy

In Hungary, developments in industrial relations at the national level are widely known: the taxi driver blockade in 1990; tripartite negotiations and agreements in the National Council for the Reconciliation of Interests; conflicts among the major trade union confederations in 1991 and 1992, and the Social Security Board elections in 1993. Much less is known about industrial relations at the enterprise level, and about the nature of relations between employers, employees and unions. What kinds of changes are occurring as a result of wider processes of economic and political transformation? What processes are occurring in large state owned enterprises, the newly-established plants of multinational companies and the growing number of small and medium-sized enterprises? In what ways is the role of trade unionism changing in these businesses; and how are the processes of management–worker relations evolving? Such questions are of utmost importance, as national level tripartism has far-reaching consequences for industrial and social peace.

This chapter examines the relationship between broader socio-economic transformation, privatization and internal restructuring of business organizations. Privatization is considered at the enterprise level, although ownership change cannot be treated separately from those national processes of marketization and economic stabilization that are driven by governmental programmes and policies. But as business organization in the emerging political democracy and market economy enjoy more autonomy, they are increasingly able to determine their own internal organizational and management structures, policies and strategies, and industrial relations. Within this context there are two funda-

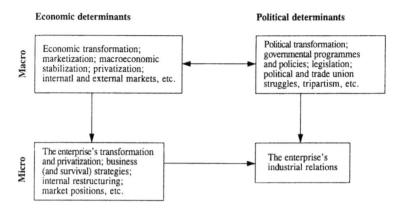

Figure 4.1 Economic and political determinants of enterprise industrial relations in Hungary.

mental questions. What is the relative importance of economic and political factors in shaping enterprise-level industrial relations; and how far does enterprise autonomy affect the nature of industrial relations?[1] The above table sets out the different factors and levels.

Privatization and industrial relations

Hungary has had its own particular method of privatization, its original philosophy being the selling of state assets to home and foreign investors (Stark 1992; Bartlett 1992). The process, having its roots in the development of small private firms in the early 1980s, was hastened by the Economic Association Act (1988) and the Transformation Act (1989). Ownership change in the state sector has had two distinct periods: until 1990 privatization was initiated and realized by the state enterprises themselves (so called "spontaneous privatization"; Marer 1992). Since 1990, when the State Property Agency (SPA) was established and transformed into a governmental agency, privatization has been controlled by the government. On the one hand the SPA's approval has been needed for privatization proposals prepared by enterprises, and on the other, the SPA has initiated and implemented privatization programmes. Technically the process is realized in such a way that in the first phase, state enterprises are transformed into economic associations (limited liability companies or share companies), and in the second phase they are sold (partly or fully) to private investors. The present (April 1994) government, when it took office (1990) envisaged the privatization of 50 per cent of state owned industry and trade by 1994. By April 1994, only 15–20 per cent of state assets had been sold to private investors. The government has also identified those enterprises that would be kept in state ownership in the long run; to control these companies, a State Property Management Holding was set up in 1992. The original philosophy of Hungarian privatization, that is, the selling of state assets, has declined somewhat recently because of difficulties in finding suitable investors and for political reasons. The three case studies discussed in this chapter are all "flagships" of the past socialist economy and they are at differing stages in the process of ownership change.

Table 4.1 Hungarian enterprises: a profile of four case study enterprises.

Enterprise	HUNGAIR	PROMED CORPN	J. V. PROTECTION	FERROCOR
Branch	Air transport	Medical equipment	Protective equipment	Steel
Number of employees	1991: 4,500	1988: 5,000	1993: 180	1990: 12,448 1993: 11,577
Ownership status	Privatized with part foreign ownership		Privatized with 50% foreign ownership	Holding company, state owned, some joint ventures

Note: J. V. Protection is a privatized division of Promed.

Promed produces medical equipment and employed about 5,000 people in its numerous plants in the 1980s. It was the first state enterprise to be transformed into an economic association, in 1988. The new organization is a holding company in which the previous enterprise retains partial ownership – together with some commercial banks – in plants which were converted into share companies. The holding company was sold to a French investor in 1990 with the joint company known as J. V. Protection. Both the Hungarian and French owners have 50–50 share ownership. Hungair (Hungarian Airlines) employs 4,500 people. Its privatization started in 1991-2, and consisted of two stages. In the first, the aviation maintenance plant was separated from the company to form the basis of a new American–Hungarian joint venture – named Aeroplex; it was to take care of Hungair's maintenance and also to attract orders from other customers. In 1992 the privatization of the air company itself started; at first it was turned into a so-called "uni-person (state) share company" and later 35 per cent of its shares were sold to Alitalia of Italy. Ferrocor, employing 11,500 people, was a typical, highly centralized, large state company until the end of the 1980s. It was the product of the rapid socialist industrialization of the 1950s, based on the development of heavy industry and steel. In 1988-9 its operating plants were transformed into limited liability companies of which the (earlier) company headquarters had full or partial ownership. It led to the creation of 46 such limited companies and other business organizations, with the holding company retaining close control over finances and investments. In 1992 the holding company was transformed into a share company in which the state remained the sole owner except for one or two joint ventures.[2] In the initial period of privatization – 1988-92 – employees, and their representative organizations, were in too weak a position to have any influence over the process (Neumann 1992; Bartlett 1992). This state of affairs was aggravated by the general uncertainties as to trade unions' rights.

According to earlier labour legislation (preceding the new Labour Code of 1992) trade unions (in fact shop steward committees) had a wide range of co-decision and consultation rights in enterprise-level decision-making with reference to working and living conditions of employees. This legislation, however, did not, and could not, take account of privatization, although its provisions were applicable in this area. Enterprise Councils – institutions of enterprise self-management including workers' representatives – were re-elected in the autumn of 1990 and continued to exist until state companies were transformed into economic associations. Enterprise Councils, at least in law, were powerful institutions: they were in a position to influence enterprises' business strategies, to elect and dismiss chief executives, etc.[3] Most Hungarian enterprises had these councils, except for those under direct control by the government such as, for example, Hungair. The Acts on Economic Associations (1988) and Transformation (1989) made no mention of workers' participation in privatization; legislation, however, prescribed Supervisory Boards for economic associations employing more than 200 people – and a third of their members were to be selected from among the representatives of workers. A government decree was issued at the end of 1991 obliging management – and the Enterprise Council – of state enterprises as well as the management of economic associations, to inform employees about privatization plans and the consequences of these for wages and welfare rights. Hence, it is clear that workers' participation in decisions concerning privatization has been guaranteed formally, at least in principle, by such institutions as shop steward committees, Enterprise Councils, Supervisory Boards and other legal provisions. In practice, wide discretionary powers have been given to those forces – the enterprise management and later the SPA – that have been in control of privatization.

Until 1990, in the period of so-called spontaneous privatization, decisions were taken at the level of the enterprise. Since 1990 – when the State Property Agency (SPA) was established – the decision-making authority has been shifted to the government, the branch ministries and the SPA. It was a contradiction of this situation that on the one hand, it was the SPA's right to decide about privatization but it was the enterprise management's (or Enterprise Council's) responsibility to keep workers fully informed.[4] The SPA could force enterprise management to do this, while the agency itself was only obliged to produce written answers to comments by trade unions and "if necessary" to receive their representatives in person. Today it is difficult to tell what guarantees, if any, have been built into the privatization process as far as its social and employment consequences are concerned (Neumann 1993). The trade unions' possibility of nominating one representative to the SPA's Board of Directors has not compensated for the very limited influence of employees.[5]

The trade unions – both those reformed and the newly-established – have taken a positive attitude towards market orientated economic change and they have regarded privatization and its social consequences – such as growing unemployment – as being inevitable. The three major confederations of labour unions have been concerned that under privatization, employees' interests should be protected in terms of employment, participation in enterprise decision-making and share ownership (Neumann 1991).

At the three companies studied as cases, it was impossible to explore to what extent (if at all) employees, i.e. trade unions, could influence transformation and privatization: direct information is extremely limited, although it was reported that there had been consultations between management and workers' representatives. However, there was some meaningful "indirect" information: on issues considered to be of importance by the national trade union confederations – such as the maintenance of employment and the opening up of possibilities for employees' stock ownership – there were signs of an impact being made by the workers' representatives. Hungair and Ferrocor maintained their employment levels during the period investigated: no mass lay-offs or significant cuts in labour took place at the two companies. When staff levels were slightly reduced, management applied techniques that were least painful for labour. At both companies, employees' stock ownership programmes have been set up through joint efforts by management and unions and approved by the State Property Agency and State Property Management Holding Company.[6]

Industrial relations: actors and institutions

In 1989–92, in the context of general political and economic change, a profound transformation of industrial relations actors and institutions took place (Héthy 1992a; Ladó 1993). Trade unions were "pluralized"; newly-formed "alternative", "independent" unions appeared on the scene (1988–9) which later united to form the Democratic League of Independent Trade Unions and MOSZ (the National Alliance of Workers' Councils). The dependence of the reformed, older unions on the party state came to an end and the monopolistic national trade union centre ceased to exist, its member organizations assuming more decentralized and democratic structures.[7] In the spring of 1990, seven trade union confederations dominated the labour scene and continue to do so up to the present: MSZOSZ (National Association of Hungarian Trade Unions); ASZOK (Autonomous Trade Unions' Confederation); SZEF (Trade Unions' Co-operation Forum); MOSZ (Workers Councils); ÉSZT (Trade Union Association of Intellectual Workers) and Solidarity.

A tripartite National Council for the Reconciliation of Interests (NCRI) was established in 1988 with the participation of labour and employer organizations and the government. At first its functions were limited to the field of wage determination but later – when confirmed by the Antall government (1990) – it was given wider authority in the formulation of public policy, the reconstruction of the industrial relations institutions and the preparation of labour legislation (Héthy (1994)). A new Labour Code (1992) – and the amendments of the old one of 1989 – dismantled those legal obstacles which had seriously hindered free collective bargaining in the previous decades.[8] The Strike Act (1989) provided the (earlier missing) regulation of collective labour disputes. These rights were coupled with new negotiating possibilities as wage determination by the state – setting strict limits for both partners in bargaining – was loosened gradually and finally abolished (1989–92). Trade unions, considered to be representative, were given the right to negotiate and conclude collective agreements on the part of labour. Works Councils, the new institutions of enterprise level workers' participation in decision-making, were set up and endowed with (mostly) consultation functions by the new Labour Code. Their actual election (May 1993), however, followed the relevant labour legislation (May 1992) with a 1 year delay. In the meantime, earlier institutions of worker participation which had been given extended authority – such as Enterprise Councils – disappeared from the scene.

The transformation of industrial relations has been burdened by political struggles: conflicts have flared up among the (new and reformed old) trade union confederations as well as between labour organizations, the government and political parties (Héthy 1992b; Deppe 1992). The seven trade union confederations joined the NCRI in 1990 and co-operated in relative peace. To co-ordinate their activities, a Trade Union Round Table was set up by them. In the spring of 1991 their relationship – primarily the contacts of MSZOSZ on one hand and the League and the Workers Councils on the other – deteriorated to the extent that the Trade Union Round Table ceased to function. The major causes of conflict were the redistribution of trade union assets and representativeness. A positive event took place as late as the autumn of 1992, when 6 major confederations came to an agreement on the partial redistribution of assets.[9] The reformed older labour organizations – primarily MSZOSZ – came into confrontation with the government in the summer of 1991, when Parliament (because of lack of agreement among the labour confederations) passed an Act about trade union assets. It obliged unions to report on their assets, sequestered these assets, blocked union funds and established a body as a provisional caretaker of these assets and funds . The intervention by the legislature was welcomed by the newly formed unions, while the traditional unions protested sharply and labelled the acts as unconstitutional and politically discriminatory. The uncertainty created by the political struggles was coupled with the uncertainty on trade union rights. In the summer of 1991 the earlier co-decision rights of unions were annulled by the Constitutional Court, while the new trade union rights were established – after much debate – as late as the spring of 1992 by the new Labour Code. The representativeness of trade unions was subjected to repeated tests by Parliament. In the summer of 1991 an Act[10] required that check-off authorizations by union members be confirmed by those members. (Traditional unions mainly applied this method to collect their membership fees.) In 1993 the elections of the trade union members of Social Security Boards as well as the elections of Works Councils took place. (In the public services, Public Servant Councils were elected.) In this process the reformed traditional unions – MSZOSZ, ASZOK, etc. – suffered certain losses, but retained their predominance, while the newly formed unions – the League and the Workers' Councils – could also prove they had a certain representativeness. In general, the trade unions' transformation (and struggles) were associated with a decline in density. But the level of unionization, estimated to be between 40 and 60 per cent in the country, could still be considered as rather high, when compared with most western European industrialized market economies.

In two of the case study companies – Hungair and Ferrocor – the national pluralization of labour organizations was reproduced, but the unions suffered only slight losses in membership. At Hungair the reformed old union survived[11] and two new unions were established. There existed also two further unions – those of pilots and stewards/ stewardesses – which did not belong to any national confederation. Similarly, at Ferrocor the old Iron Workers Union – affiliated with MSZOSZ – continued to function, while local organizations of the League, the Workers' Councils and Solidarity were established. It was a particular feature of this company that the Youth Organization – a successor of the (past) Communist Youth Organization – also survived as a union: it had members who belonged simultaneously to other unions. In the Promed plant there existed only one labour organization, which belonged to the Iron Workers' Federation (and MSZOSZ).

The establishment of new trade unions at the enterprises seem to follow three possible scenarios (Kameniczky 1992): (a) employees join to form a new union at the same time as the old union ceases to exist; (b) new labour organizations are formed among a definite group of employees or organizational unit with well-defined interests of their own, while the old union survives in other groups or units; and (c) a new union appears on the scene but the old union also continues to function and often retains its predominance. For co-operation among the individual labour organizations, the third version is the most critical and conflictual. It was by following this last scenario that the pluralization of workers' representation began at both Hungair and Ferrocor. At these two large companies the establishment of new unions reflected the strategies of their national confederations[12] – beyond the local initiative – to obtain footholds in business organizations which were well known and in this way to build up public support. Such strategies seem reasonable since the new trade unions start to function in a disadvantageous position – compared with the older ones – because of their limited human, organizational and financial resources. They can only hope to succeed by concentrating their limited resources on well-chosen battlefields. At J. V. Protection, no alternative labour organizations appeared as there was no local initiative to organize them. The local Iron Workers Union retained its monopoly to represent workers' interests, but the level of unionization, unlike in the two other companies, declined sharply – from 85–90 per cent to 25 per cent – with managers and white-collar workers leaving.

In May 1993, Works Council elections took place in Hungarian companies. These elections had a double importance. They made it possible for unions to demonstrate their representativeness, since at enterprise level it was necessary for unions – according to the law – to obtain 10 per cent of the votes. This was also a precondition for the availability of certain trade union rights – such as the protection of trade union officers. Secondly, they opened up the possibility for representative trade union(s) to enter into collective negotiations and to participate in collective agreements. To be eligible for this, union(s) had to obtain 50 per cent of the total votes or Works Council seats.[13] MSZOSZ-affiliated unions proved to be most successful at each of the three companies, such that they were able to participate in collective agreements; newly-formed unions often failed to obtain 10 per cent of the votes. At Ferrocor the votes obtained by each of the unions were: Iron Workers Union, 80.3 per cent; Youth Organization, 11.3 per cent; Workers' Councils, 3.2 per cent; Commercial and Financial Workers Union, 0.7 per cent; and independent candidates, 4.5 per cent. In Hungair's five Works Councils, four were controlled by candidates of the reformed old union. At J. V. Protection the Works Council was dominated by the Iron Workers Union.

The success of MSZOSZ – and its member organizations – created a special position for trade unions. It became obvious that bargaining rights would be exercised by labour organizations relying on a developed national structure, a national network of activists, and on considerable experience in public policy formulation. In this way employers would be engaging in collective bargaining with the same union, so that there would be a very limited chance that one union could be played off against another. Indeed, it strengthened the possibilities for co-ordinating workers' representation and participation.

But what level of influence can be achieved through workers' participation taking into account Works Councils' relatively weak, mainly consultative,[14] legal authority and how successful can unions be in the process of collective bargaining? In each of the three companies no new collective agreements were concluded during the period investigated. There were negotiations, but older collective agreements, which had been agreed within the framework of the previous state-owned enterprises, remained in force. These collective contracts, which had been signed hurriedly in view of future privatization, had provided better protection for workers against dismissals – in terms of severance pay and length of period of notice – than current labour legislation. It had been usual for unions to insist upon such guarantees, which also protected the interests of managers. In the collective negotiations in 1992 there were efforts by senior managers, both at Hungair and Ferrocor, to reduce provisions in the collective agreements to the minimum standards of labour law.[15] Instead of wider collective agreements, only "narrow" annual agreements on wage levels were concluded.

The enterprises: economic situation, conflicts and co-operation

In 1991–2 all three of the case study companies were economically viable. Hungair was successful in exploiting opportunities offered by international politics, obtaining an important share in the transport of Jewish emigrants to Israel from the former USSR. It continued to fly to the Middle East during the Gulf War and it earned profits on the purchase of cheap Soviet kerosene. J. V. Protection also obtained orders because of the Gulf War which made possible for it to sell its stocks and boost, if only provisionally, its production. Ferrocor, as the country's technologically most developed steel works producing good quality products, could sell both at home – after its rivals collapsed – and abroad. This success, however, proved to be short-lived, because of a transitory boom and had little to do with efforts to overcome basic structural problems. In 1993 Hungair was in serious deficit and Ferrocor was also faced with grave financial difficulties, as a result of the recession in western Europe and the Yugoslav trade embargo.

For the companies, three interrelated economic processes set challenges which called for profound structural change: (a) marketization; (b) recession; and (c) privatization. By marketization is meant the elimination of earlier subsidies and protection by the state, and exposure to the impact of market forces. The Hungarian market was opened up for imports, price and wage determination was considerably liberalized, and state subsidies cut. In this context business organizations got rid of administrative obstacles in price setting: they became free to realize their costs in their sales, but they were largely prevented from doing so because of growing competition. The decline in home demand and the collapse of COMECON trade with the former socialist countries, coupled with the recession in western Europe, affected manufacturing, engineering and the steel industry heavily. Economic processes within the country – the fall in GDP and industrial output[16] – were also driven by the fiscal policies of governments aimed at macroeconomic stabilization (OECD 1993). Strategies of survival pursued by the three enterprises were different, but they had some similarities. There was a general effort to adapt to the market, to improve the quality of products and services, to develop marketing activities, to involve Western know-how, and to achieve technological development. Organizational changes – in fact, decentralization and disintegration – primarily at Promed and Ferrocor, encouraged a stronger profit orientation and cost effectiveness of operating units. All three companies attempted to attract foreign capital: for Ferrocor it was considered to be important for its programme of technological development, and for Hungair it was necessary to modernize its fleet of aircraft. Promed hoped for know-how and markets from its French co-owner, while for Hungair the involvement of a foreign investor promised, beyond new purchases and management methods, a "marriage" which could provide competitive size in the international market. During these changes, relations between management and unions differed in each of the three companies.

At Hungair, relations between management and unions oscillated between periods of conflict and co-operation. At the same time, relations between the individual unions were seriously burdened by rivalry and competition to prove their militant determination to represent workers. The position of the individual unions, those affiliated with MSZOSZ, the League and those non-affiliated, were strong and relatively balanced. Of the 3,500 trade union members – the level of unionization was 80 per cent – "only" 1,500 belonged to the traditional union, with the rest supporting other labour organizations. There were a number of disputed issues.

(i) The establishment of an American–Hungarian joint venture
Employers and trade unions were concerned about several problems. What chance would the joint venture have in the market if its creation did not involve technological development and related capital investment? What would be the consequences of the joint venture on work and working conditions? Workers were alarmed by the possibility that Aeroplex would be engaged in less qualified and lower paid work tasks, such as the repair of aircraft bodies, because of outdated technological equipment. And what impact would the joint venture have on the wages of employees? Trade union demands probably played a positive role in the resolution of such problems. Only a slight reduction of the labour force has taken place and the joint venture's employees have been given the opportunity to buy Hungair shares.

(ii) The reorganization and rationalization of the air company
Hungair's general director (appointed in 1990) was aware of the need for redundancies and he had in mind a figure of about 15 per cent. The trade unions were worried that management would proceed with this without proper consultation and that the whole process would disregard the differing conditions of the separate organizational units and would not result in an overall improvement in the quality of the company's labour force. Tensions between management and unions became acute, with the general director blaming the unions for jeopardizing the company's survival changes, while the unions retorted by attacking the management as "incompetent". However, any mass lay-offs have been deferred and in 1993 there was a planned staff reduction of 4 per cent.

(iii) Employee and trade union rights
Disputes over labour rights have occurred in great numbers since 1990 at Hungair. In 1992 one trade union protested against the "excessive

transgression" of flying time limits in the case of stewardesses. Management, however, claimed that there were no such complaints on the part of the employees, and that the "excessive transgression" referred to one occasion when a stewardess, on a voluntary basis, undertook additional flight duty to substitute an absent colleague. The same union also demanded the retraining of all stewardesses for service on Boeing 767 planes, to provide them with adequate skills; however, at the same time management argued that many stewardesses were unwilling to undertake long distance flights. There has been a long catalogue of such minor disputes including issues of workers' participation. One of the Works Councils, shortly after its election in the Autumn of 1993, took the general director to court for his decision to close the company's holiday house at Lake Balaton for the winter and, accordingly, to dismiss the staff, without previous consultations with the Works Council. In the Council's views it had consultative rights on this issue. The company's management employed a qualified labour lawyer, a former labour court judge, as a human resource manager to deal with such disputes and to resist employee demands.

(iv) Wage increases

Collective disputes about wages started as early as 1990–1 but they led to industrial action only in 1993. The first wage negotiation of the American–Hungarian joint venture took place in the summer of 1991. It was initiated not by the trade union but directly by the employees. The workers, worrying about their overtime bonuses and secondary jobs, engaged in direct negotiations with the Hungarian/American management and agreed that the annual wage growth would be 21 per cent. At Hungair itself, although threats of strike action were repeatedly made in the earlier years, the first warning strike took place in the summer of 1993, after the privatization of the company. The pilots demanded a 70 per cent annual wage increase while the rest of the staff asked for 50 per cent; they later reduced their claims and were granted somewhat less than half they had demanded.[17] Such groups of employees have proved to be successful in their fight for higher wages even when over-employment is well-known and when their position in the labour market is not strong. At Aeroplex, a second term of wage negotiations followed in the summer of 1993, leading to similar results. In the first stage the union demanded almost a 200 per cent wage increase for the coming 18-month period; and the final agreement – after a three day strike – fixed a 35 per cent increase. This industrial action was the first important strike at a joint venture; the workers' demands were strongly resisted by Hungair management, who brought in Ukrainian and British maintenance workers to break the action.[18]

At Ferrocor, co-operation and continuity have deeper roots than confrontation and change. The level of unionization has remained at 80–90 per cent. The Iron Workers' Union – affiliated with MSZOSZ – having 7,000 members out of 11,500 employees. The membership of other unions – those of the League, the Workers' Councils and Solidarity – was no more than 1–200 members each. At first, in 1990–1, their small size seemed to be compensated for by their "voice", and by the militant attitude of their leaders. They attacked the Iron Workers' Union sharply on political and ideological grounds. But later, as the national positions of the reformed older unions became consolidated, the Iron Workers' Union became more active, making use of its organization, activists, networks, experience and resources. In this period the trade unions' attitude towards management was determined basically by the moderate and co-operative policies of the Iron Workers' Union. Ferrocor has been free of debates and conflicts between employers and unions such as those which led to industrial action at its Austrian–Hungarian joint venture, Ferrocor Mountain. Most debates have concentrated on wages. Actual wage increases, however, have regularly surpassed negotiated wage deals; the rates of increase being 24.5 per cent in 1991 and 25.4 per cent in 1992, while the negotiated rates were 20 per cent and 22 per cent respectively. In a similar way, negotiated minimum wage levels have slightly exceeded the national guaranteed minimum wage: in 1993 it was fixed at 9,500 HUF per month while the national minimum was 9,000 HUF per month. The management has maintained social welfare benefits and if such measures assist only small groups of workers, they can be interpreted as being a positive gesture.

In the development of trade union strategies, managerial attitudes are important. Hungair's general director, appointed to his position in 1990, was determined to pursue reorganization and rationalization plans – including envisaged mass lay-offs – regardless of the resistance of employees and trade unions. He firmly believed that such changes were absolutely necessary to maintain the viability of the company and he had the full support of the owner (i.e. the Ministry). The general director was disillusioned, however, when, after a one-year period, he had to resign. His attitude had outraged trade union leaders so much that they used all possible means of opposition, from political demagogy[19] to personal attacks against top managers. They accused the managers of corruption and an official investigation was even set up. The general director himself was not reserved in his attitudes; he threatened disciplinary procedures. By contrast, in Ferrocor – although the "paternalist" general director of the earlier period was removed in 1990 – the past traditions of "taking care of the workers", and of close co-operation with labour unions seems to have continued. To prove his willingness to co-operate, the new general director refrained from attempting to change the collective agreement that had been signed by his predecessor, although the economic environment of the enterprise had deteriorated rapidly. From the point of view of its relations with employees and unions, management's efforts to maintain the level of employment were of utmost importance. The number in the labour force decreased only slightly during the period 1990-3, from 12,500 to 11,500. This reduction has been realized by means which are least painful to the workers: by the termination of employment of foreign labour, by reducing overtime, by administrative limitations on hiring new employees, and by early retirement. At J. V. Protection, although there is a trade union, there exists no articulate trade union strategy. The labour organization has not been involved with rationalization processes and labour force reduction: the number of employees decreased from 260 in 1988 to 180 in 1992. The major guarantee for the representation of workers' interests has been the "paternalist" attitude of the management, and primarily of the chief executive. He has made repeated efforts to maintain the delicate balance between the French owner's demands for reduction in production costs, and the tolerance of employees. As the workers' aspirations concerning their wages and income are mainly satisfied and they have relative job security, the chief executive is a generally respected key figure in the company's industrial relations.

When Hungair and Ferrocor are compared, "conflictual" and "co-operative" industrial relations can be distinguished. However, the dividing line between the two are not always clear. It is true that sharp, open and public conflicts are primarily a characteristic of Hungair, but one should not forget that such clashes have been temporary and short-term. In the first half of 1992, when the new general director submitted future plans to a trade union meeting in order to get reactions from workers' representatives, none of his plans were challenged. The event had been preceded by a joint declaration of the seven Hungair trade unions in August 1991, which had criticized the (resigned) general director sharply: for serious negligence (or even misconduct) in his relations with employees; for grave violations of labour law; for the exclusion of unions from information vital for their effective functioning; and for the generation of a climate of uncertainty over mass lay-offs. This first co-ordinated action by trade unions led the management to recognize the importance of workers' representatives and of negotiations with them. It reacted by initiating dialogue about the most pressing topical issues, and the general director also decided to receive two representatives from each union on the first Thursday of each month to "promote a better flow of information".

At Hungair and Ferrocor, managements in the new pluralized trade union situation did not refuse dialogue with them, although the general political climate and the uncertainties of their position could have led to this. Instead, they maintained contact with all labour organizations without marked preferences; there were no efforts to discriminate or to eliminate any of the unions in the companies. Institutions for dialogue with workers' representatives (so-called "local interest reconciliation bodies"), following the example of the National Council for the Reconciliation of Interests (NCRI) were set up and operated at both companies. However, their functions were limited to information and consultation. At Hungair the process of "reconciliation of interests" was meant to have several levels and to respond to the hierarchy of decision-making. However, there is little evidence to suggest that this worked effectively. At both companies, despite periods of rivalry and clashes among the labour organizations, there were efforts to unite for joint and co-ordinated action. To promote this, Ferrocor unions established a Council of Interest Protection, while Hungair unions created a Trade Union Round Table – both being trade union bodies. At the steel company the unions concluded an agreement to secure the fairness of Works Council elections.[20] In August 1991 a "crisis committee" was set up at the air company to exercise joint pressure on management. At both companies there was a more or less effective co-operation among unions in the bodies of "reconciliation of interests" – following the example and the spirit of the NCRI.

In Hungary, enterprise-level industrial relations of past decades had been characterized by management/trade union co-operation and by a lack of conflict in the sense that strikes had rarely occurred. If they had, they had occured despite the disapproval of labour organizations.[21] In 1988–92 the pillars of such co-operation collapsed because of governmental economic and social policies, the institutional framework of industrial relations and labour legislation, and industrial relations philosophies and ideologies.[22] New possibilities opened up for both co-operative and conflictual industrial relations within enterprises. The old and new trade unions were candidates for both roles. But what are those conditions which lead to the survival of co-operation at enterprise level, even if in a modified form? Clearly, the challenge of enterprise survival is important. In the context of privatization a lack of joint co-ordinated efforts endangers both management and trade unions. Equally, the old (and new) managements and unions are faced with a weakening in their legitimacy. Both of them have to prove that they are able to cope with new difficulties and an obvious approach to this is to find solutions by joint efforts. Open conflicts, on the other hand, when the companies are faced with grave economic difficulties, can be detrimental to the company's market position. At the same time, senior management and trade union leadership – the majority of which had been trained in the earlier system – are instinctively co-operative and they evade conflicts.[23] Furthermore, national level industrial relations have an impact; they are mainly co-operative, and management, unions and government continue to co-operate in the NCRI despite all the conflicts which occurred in their relationships in 1991–2.

Economic and political pressure

Industrial relations within enterprises seem to reflect the interrelated and controversial influence of both economic and political factors. At the same time, autonomous developments depending on the characteristics of particular companies, and their industrial relations practices, seem to have growing importance. The increased autonomy of business organizations indicates the gradual extrication of their industrial relations from external political and ideological pressures. Economic determination, that is, the impact of societal transformation and privatization on enterprise level industrial relations, seems basically to be indirect. Ownership change in itself – the substitution of the state as owner by quasi-private or private owners – does not necessarily result in the transformation of industrial relations. Structural changes in production, technology, organization and employment – initiated by or speeded up by ownership change – are more likely to be the factors that reshape relations between employers and employees. The trade unions' position, according to international experience,[24] is very much dependent upon such structural developments. The direct impact of ownership change – such as the industrial relations philosophy of new owners and their attitude towards labour organizations may be felt, but it seems to be of minor importance. The question is: to what extent does transformation and privatization lead to (or follow) inevitable structural changes which were needed in the former state-owned socialist enterprises to secure their survival?

At the three companies (before their transformation and privatization) large stock surpluses had accumulated involving heavy costs. At J. V. Protection, due to its quasi-military production, such surpluses had existed in the capacity of machinery, stocks, buildings, land and, above all, employment. Ferrocor and Hungair had similar surpluses. In this context it is interesting that only J. V. Protection – the only company behaving as a genuine private enterprise – has started to eliminate its stock surpluses and to cut its costs, while the other two quasi-private or state-owned companies have in the main maintained their earlier practices.[25] At Ferrocor and Hungair the maintenance of over-employment has been a major basis for co-operation between management and unions. Management, feeling insecure in its position, is hesitant to introduce redundancies. Such a move was seen by them as premature until it was made necessary by ownership change and economic constraints. Steel production and aviation are highly capital-intensive activities, so wage costs are relatively low, and the reduction of wages could not remedy the two companies' financial troubles. Employment is also a sensitive political issue. Ferrocor provided jobs for a medium-sized Hungarian town, while Hungair's labour force, particularly its middle management and administrative staff, traditionally have good political connections. Both companies were also dependent on the government, with managers appointed by state agencies, and their Supervisory Boards and Boards of Directors dominated by political nominees. Internal structural changes at both Ferrocor and Hungair led to only gradual cuts in employment. Ferrocor's disintegration into a set of "quasi-independent", limited liability firms functioning as profit centres can be looked upon as a first step towards rationalization. Serious debates take place among these companies about internal prices. At Hungair, although very few effective

changes have occurred in the core business, the separation of the maintenance unit and its conversion into a joint venture is an initial step towards
rationalization.

Such structural changes have had an impact on industrial relations
because they involve a decentralization or separation of employers'
functions. J. V. Protection has become completely independent as far as
industrial relations is concerned. A similar change has taken place at
Hungair with the establishment of Aeroplex, except that in this case the
parent company – in its capacity as co-owner – has continued to play an
active role in industrial relations. At Ferrocor, the company's headquarters has retained its "co-ordinating functions" in the field of industrial
relations, with the aim of maintaining parity between the limited liability
companies in terms of wage levels. In this, it has relied on the collective
"framework" agreement, which covers all its firms, and makes use of its
own Works Council.[26]

Political determination has also had an impact upon company-level
industrial relations developments. First, the government has had an
active and decisive role in the process of enterprise transformation and
privatization. Secondly, in the initial phase of privatization, the state
has continued to function as the major employer of labour. Thirdly,
struggles in national industrial relations – having an impact on enterprises – have been politically motivated and closely interrelated with
political struggles. Fourthly, legislation reshaping industrial reactions
was born within a process of political decision-making. Managers, trade
union activists and employees – even if they were not fully aware of such
determination – acted under the shadow of politics. The possession of
political power, and the major directions of political change, were
decided by the 1990 elections. However, there were grave tensions in
the relationship between the government and the trade unions. While in
the political arena the governing conservative coalition was faced with a
liberal and socialist opposition, in the trade union arena the reformed old
and the newly established workers' organizations were opposed to each
other. The most important trade union confederations had links with the
political parties in opposition, but the governing coalition had no such
partners on the unions' side that shared its political and ideological
values and rendered support.[27] This situation, and the lack of clear
industrial relations philosophies, explain the uncertainties and contradictions of the government's attitude towards the trade unions (Héthy
1993). These policies are double-edged; both pragmatic and at the same

time ideological. It was pragmatism which made the government revive the tripartite National Council of the Reconciliation of Interests in the summer of 1990, to engage in talks with all the existing trade union confederations in this body, and in this way to accept *de facto* them as legitimate and representative. Negotiations in the NCRI were continued even in the period of sharp confrontation between the government and unions (1991-2). At the same time, the government intervened in trade union affairs and subjected the labour organizations to repeated tests of legitimacy and representativeness. These measures were not free of ideological and political motivation. It is a challenging task for political analysts to discover how the political pressure exercised by the government contributed to the consolidation of the workers' organizations in 1993, with MSZOSZ retaining its predominance among them. The explanation for the success of MSZOSZ at a national level, and of its affiliates within the companies investigated, is partly because of its internal reforms and efforts. But these workers' organizations could not, and did not, become "genuine trade unions" overnight. Their public support originated from the general political mood as well as from the past experiences of employees. The old reformed trade unions' co-operative behaviour, even if it was in a sense a direct continuation of past practices, seemed to fit more adequately the present conditions of state-controlled transformation than did alternative confrontational attitudes, based upon abstract market economy ideals, with which the newly formed unions hoped to attract members and supporters.

Perspectives – before and after privatization

Privatization is a complex process; even the concept itself is ambiguous. In a wider sense, it indicates the development of the private sector. It has two major components. First, the establishment of new privately owned firms; and, second, it involves the transfer of state assets to private owners. New privately owned companies are mainly small undertakings – the number of which has been growing rapidly – but they also include big "greenfield" investments by multinationals such as Ford and Suzuki. The establishment of new undertakings usually relies on capital investment. Here, state assets function as capital, as in the case of the joint ventures of Hungair and Ferrocor. Privatization, in a narrower sense, indicates the selling of state owned enterprises to private investors. From the point of industrial relations, the process of privatization seems to be important because in newly established private firms there are genuine private owner(s) and a management dependent on them. The privatization of state owned enterprises, on the contrary, often leads to quasi-private ownership – partial or full state ownership – with a politically dependent management. Newly established private firms are free to decide, within the limits set by labour legislation, how to set up their industrial relations systems but privatized state-owned companies have a legacy of industrial relations. The companies investigated in our case studies represent a particular group of firms from the aspect of privatization. They are large, state-owned companies in which the state's ownership has been partly or fully maintained. They are, however, in differing phases of privatization and internal restructuring. J. V. Protection seems to be a genuine private company, under the control of a foreign owner and with the Hungarian management dependent upon the owner. Hungair's (partial) privatization was undertaken during the period of our research but the state maintained its majority ownership despite having an Italian investor, Alitalia. At Ferrocor privatization, except for its joint ventures, is a possible option for the future. It is an open question, taking into consideration the international recession in the steel industry and the company's debts, whether it can be sold at all. These differing stages and ways of privatization have affected the nature of industrial relations developments in each of the three companies. At J. V. Protection a "silent disintegration" of collective industrial relations[28] has taken place. Formally, the collective model has continued to exist, but substantively it has been replaced by managerial paternalism, and the future of the trade union seems to be doubtful. At Hungair industrial relations developments, after privatization, have entered an exciting phase. The trade unions and the collective model seem to be consolidated and, at the same time, interests of employees are articulated clearly and represented effectively – as indicated by the work stoppages of 1993. At present, trade unions are in a position to take the initiative and conflicts are frequent. Ferrocor's privatization and future is burdened by uncertainties. Collective industrial relations continue to exist and relations between management and unions can be described as "pragmatic co-operation" or "mutual tolerance". This model will probably continue until radical changes occur in the position of the company.

In research relying on case studies, the generalization of findings is always a major dilemma. In 1992 the Japan Institute of Labour, in co-operation with the Hungarian Labour Research Institute, carried out a survey about company-level industrial relations in 446 large Hungarian enterprises. According to its results, the major difficulties the enterprises were facing were shrinking markets (94 per cent), the collapse of COMECON trade (32 per cent), and the lack of capital (70 per cent). Companies' solutions to these problems included changes in business policies (78 per cent), reductions in the labour force (75 per cent), reorganization (72 per cent), and speeding up of privatization (67 per cent). Transformation into economic associations was completed or under way in 70 per cent of these enterprises. Most firms (85 per cent) had trade unions; MSZOSZ member organizations were present in 70 per cent of the companies. Where workers' representation was pluralized, the unions made efforts to maintain an often "institutionalized" dialogue. Management in such cases had contacts with all the unions and there were no signs of discriminatory policies. At several firms local bodies were set up for the "reconciliation of interests". The managers, according to their own reports, consulted workers' representatives in the most critical issues of organizational transformation such as mass lay-offs and privatization. Wages and social benefits remained a focus of labour disputes and a growing concern was job security. Labour disputes rarely led to industrial action: strikes occurred in only 13 per cent of the firms (Japan Institute of Labour 1993).

A major question for the future is whether subsequent phases of organizational transformation and privatization necessarily result in the process we have described at the three companies. Will the collective models of industrial relations of Ferrocor, Hungair and other state owned or quasi-private companies – after privatization is completed – be substituted by "quasi-collective" or "individualized" models? In other words, is the "silent disintegration" of collective industrial relations – as found at J. V. Protection – an inevitable perspective of the future? In certain groups of firms there is a possibility that trade unions will disappear – or fail to organize membership – and individual-based bargaining relations prevail.[29] Such a danger is related to the appearance and increasing influence of multinational companies and of investors with an interest in short-term profit maximization, supported by strong political forces.[30] Even if there is such a trend, investors' industrial relations philosophies may not always be hostile to collective bargaining. Further, Hungarian management has an important role, both before and after privatization, in shaping management–trade union relations. The consolidation of labour relations actors, institutions and labour legislation also sets limits to voluntary actions on the part of employers. However, our empirical knowledge of enterprise-level industrial relations is too limited to provide a well-founded general description. Clearly, no standard model seems to exist and industrial relations among enterprises is characterized by a wide variety of forms, their patterns differing within various groups of firms. Such differences are related to the gradual extrication of firms from the stranglehold of politics and ideology, while developments in industrial relations are characterized by both continuity and change. Privatization and related organizational restructuring seem to be major forces shaping the changing relationship between employers and employees, but this process, as yet, has not had its full impact. As such, future developments, particularly in view of the election results in May 1994, remain, as always, uncertain.

Notes

1. The case studies have been prepared by Gy. Kaucsek (Hungair), P. Simon (Ferrocor), F. Ternovszky and M. Adorján (J. V. Protection).
2. Compare the transformation (and privatization) process of Ferrocor with those of another giant Hungarian steel industry, Lenin Metallurgical Works (Burawoy & Lukács 1992).
3. For the rights of Enterprise Councils see: Governmental Decree No 33/1984 (31 November) on the Implementation of Act No VI/1977 on State Enterprises. Törvények és Rendeletek Hivatalos Gyûjteménye. I. kötet. Közgazdasági és Jogi K. Budapest, 1985. 251–8. For a detailed description see: Héthy and Csuhaj (1990). Enterprise Councils had employee representatives but were dominated by managers (Héthy 1988).
4. According to Governmental Decree No 119/1991, the management's duty was fulfilled if the plan for the transformation and privatization of the enterprise had been endorsed by the employees' representatives before its submission to the SPA.
5. The privatization process has evaded social control in general: SPA decisions could not be disputed in court and all parliamentary efforts to control the SPA have met with failure.
6. A 5 per cent share of the basic capital of 7.5 HUF was reserved (by the State Property Management Holding) for stocks available for employees; the selling price of the stocks is fixed at 200 per cent of the face value, which is reduced, however, by 50 per cent; a further privilege for employees is that they have to pay

only 25 per cent of the price immediately; the time period for full payment is fixed at three years (the credit interests, however, is lower than that of the National Bank). Stocks also can be purchased in exchange for so-called "compensation vouchers" (accepted at their face value plus interest). The employees' stocks' circulation is limited: for a 5 year period the State Property Management Holding has the right to repurchase the stocks if they are sold. Employees are entitled to buy stocks to a limit of the annual sum of their wages or salaries, with a maximum of 140,000 HUF. (The minimum limit is fixed at 40,000 HUF.) Hungair trade unions fought for a somewhat higher ratio (10 per cent) of employee shares in the capital so that they could delegate a representative to the Board of Directors, and for more favourable conditions.

7. Decentralization included disposal of financial resources. Ferrocor trade union membership fees (representing 1 per cent of wages and salaries) are divided as follows: 50 per cent remains with the local trade union organization, 10 per cent are transferred to the strike fund and 10 per cent to insurance, while 30 per cent is paid to the branch federation of Iron Workers (10 per cent of which goes to MSZOSZ).

8. Munkatörvénykönyv, 1992. évi XXII. Törvény. (Labour Code, Act No. XXII. 1992) Magyar Közlöny. 1992. május 4. In English: Labour Law Documents, ILO, Geneva, No. 1. 1993.

9. The confederation Solidarity refused to join the agreement. Solidarity was later also excluded from the NCRI by the other confederations, because of its extremist policies.

10. At Ferrocor, 99 per cent of the trade union membership renewed their authorizations, but this ratio was lower at the other two companies.

11. The Hungair trade unions were cautious about revealing their affiliations openly: by this secrecy they probably tried to evade biases in politics and public opinion.

12. Developments seem to indicate that the new trade unions had limited interest in declining economic branches (such as metallurgy, mining), while their primary targets were those with solid perspectives (such as transport).

13. Until the Works Council elections, all trade unions were provided with the right of bargaining and signing collective agreements under the interim legislation.

14. The Works Council, as regulated by the Labour Code, is endowed with co-decision right in two issues: (i) the disposal of social welfare funds and assets (as regulated in the collective agreement); and (ii) the regulation of labour safety.

15. In the first half of 1993 there existed 380 enterprise level collective agreements covering 580,000 employees. (The numbers are roughly equal to those of 1992.) 60 per cent of these agreements (in terms of the number of enterprises) contained provisions for average wage growth, and 80 per cent for the growth of basic wages. (The rate of negotiated wage growth averaged about 16–17 per cent; it was in line with forecasts to the increase in consumer prices but would be clearly inferior as to the actual rate of inflation); 40 per cent of the agreements provided for a minimum wage above the legal guaranteed minimum (on average 10 per cent) and regulated wage scales. In manufacturing, 35 per cent of the employees were covered by collective agreements; this ratio was much higher – at about 70

per cent – in transport, telecommunications and postal services, dominated mainly by big companies. (Ministry of Labour 1993).

16. GDP and industrial output have declined continuously since 1990 and 1989 respectively. In 1991 GDP dropped 11.9 per cent, and that of industrial output by 19.1 per cent.

17. The pilots' demand was interpreted by the press and mass media as a claim for western European wages. What they in fact asked for was a correction in the hierarchy of wages: they demanded a second place for themselves after top management, as was the practice – they argued – in Western air companies.

18. Hungair's general director described the industrial action at the mother company as "disciplined and moderate", while the workers of Aeroplex – in his view – resorted to the final weapon too early and confused their partners by calling for unlimited strikes (interview 1993).

19. When Aeroplex was established, the trade unions tried to transform what was basically economic into a political matter; in a public statement they raised the question: "In whose interest is it to place Hungary's most important aircraft maintenance base into foreign hands? In our view, it is not a simple issue of business, but one of national security."

20. They agreed upon certain mutually acceptable rules, such as: they would not conclude special agreements to defeat others; they would refrain from negative campaigning; they would suspend the recruitment of new members in the campaign period; they would engage in positive propaganda for the Works Council and for their own organization; they would limit the number of their candidates so that the validity of the elections would be guaranteed; on the day of voting even written propaganda would be suspended; possible disputes among them would be settled by negotiations within three days; and possible violations of their agreement would be made public.

21. This situation is well illustrated by the case of slow-downs and work stoppages at RABA (Hungarian Railway Carriage and Machine Works)(Héthy & Makó 1989).

22. The major guarantees of such co-operative relations were as follows: (a) job security and continuous (also modest) real wage growth (interrupted by years of decline) were taken care of by governmental economic policies; at the same time initiatives by the employers and trade unions were limited (primarily by administrative wage determination by the state); (b) legislation on industrial relations was supposed to promote co-operation between management and unions: it favoured co-operative workers' participation to conflictual collective bargaining, providing considerable rights in the first field (e.g. for Enterprise Councils) and limiting rights in the second; (c) institutionalized (formal) bargaining, however, was replaced by non-institutionalized (informal) bargaining, at least by certain groups of labour in strong bargaining positions: from 1982 the government made efforts to institutionalize (formalize) these (informal) transactions within the institutions of entrepreneurship, within and outside the enterprises; (d) in official ideology, the concepts of "workers' ownership", of "higher level interests uniting both workers and managers", and of the "common interests of socialist construction" were also intended to confirm this co-operation. (For the changes, see:

105

Makó 1992).

23. On the side of the unions, such an attitude was perceived in the textile industry. [The Textile Workers' Union] "has sent out letters to test its local organizations as to their attitudes concerning negotiations about guaranteed minimum wages. The answers were as if given by employers: a growth in minimum wages is unwanted as it would add to unemployment, it would risk the bankruptcy of the company, it would contribute to wage distortions etc. There was a textile company where the minimum wage had not been raised to the legally guaranteed level of 8,000 HUF/month and nothing happened . . . The attitudes of other unions outside of MSZOSZ did not differ" (Orolin 1992).

24. The decline in the level of unionization, as is widely known, can be attributed to such structural changes as the growth of small and medium-sized enterprises (SMEs), the growth of employment in services and its decline in traditional industries, technological development and the reduction of classical manual jobs, the spread of atypical work (part-time work), etc.

25. The transformation of state property into quasi-private property is evaluated by M. Tardos (1992) as follows: "The process of so-called 'spontaneous privatization' whereby state firms are transformed into state-owned partnerships is positive in that the market value of the capital is determined, dividends are paid on shares, and proprietors have clear expectations. Transformation has created however a system of cross ownership between state firms, where the new proprietors, the leading managers of the joint stock or limited liability company, and the employers are all interested in converting the firm's capital into personal income and in consuming it."

26. Works Councils, according to the Labour Code of 1992, can be established in those units of the enterprises where the management was endowed with employer's rights. In this way in the big limited liability companies of Ferrocor, Works Councils were elected on two hierarchical levels. A Works Council was also elected at the headquarters: as this had no employer's rights over the employees of the limited liability companies, its Works Council could not be provided with general co-ordinating functions.

27. Among the trade union confederations, MOSZ (Workers' Councils) had the closest links with the government (and the major coalition party, the Hungarian Democratic Forum); its efforts to promote workers' self management – following the example of the short-lived Workers' Councils of 1956 – collided, however, with the privatization philosophy of the government. In 1992 there was a (politically motivated) attempt to set up a Christian trade union confederation (KESZOSZ); it participated in the Social Security Boards' elections, but was not accepted by the other confederations as a member of the NCRI.

28. Collective industrial relations mean that the employment relationship is based on a collective contract (concluded by the employer and the trade union); in individualized industrial relations the employment relationship – in the absence of a collective agreement and usually of a trade union – is based on individual work contracts.

29. Industrial relations of various groups of firms differ considerably; a major fea-

ture of small private undertakings including joint ventures, according to the information at our disposal, is the absence of trade unions (and collective bargaining). A 1991 survey of 165 joint ventures found that only 8 per cent had unions (Kaucsek 1992). The local plants of multinationals pursue very different practices as dictated by the philosophy of their management, by their legacy, etc. Some of them, for example, have no trade unions (Ford, Levi's, McDonald's), while labour organizations are present at others (Tungsram–General Electric, Hungarian Suzuki, GM–Hungaria, etc.)(Neumann 1993).

30. Csákó lists the following major obstacles to positive developments: (a) institutions have been established on the basis of theoretical and political considerations having little to do with actual industrial relations practices; (b) the new strong economic actors enjoying political support are opposed to the democratization of industrial relations; and (c) people are suspicious about their institutionalized representation and fears of powerful bureaucracies have deep roots in their thinking (Csákó 1992). However, on the basis of our own research project and other studies I cannot share Csákó's general pessimism about the future of industrial relations.

Appendix   The position of trade union confederations in Hungary.

Confederation	Membership (April 1991) ('000)	Membership (Spring 1993) ('000)	Social Security Board elections (May 1993)				Works Council–Public Servant Council Elections (May 1993)	
			Health Insurance Board Votes (%)	Seats	Pension Insurance Board Votes(%)	Seats	Works Councils Votes (%)[b]	Public Servant Councils Votes (%)[b]
MSZOSZ	2,683[a]	1,200	45.2	15	50.1	18	71.7	9.4
SZEF	557	550	8.4	2	10.6	3	–	49.1
ASZOK	374	410	5.3	1	4.8	1	18.6	0.5
The League	130	250	13.1	4	10.1	3	5.7	4.9
MOSZ (Workers Councils)	160	160	12.8	4	10.9	3	2.2	0.2
ÉSZT	63	110	6.8	2	6.2	2	1.0	7.2
Solidarity	75	–	–	–	–	–	–	–
KESZOSZ	–	–	8.4	2	7.3	2	–	–

Notes: a) After the renewal of check-off authorizations (1991 Autumn), MSZOSZ reported 1.9 million members. b) The rest of the votes were received by candidates of non-affiliated unions and independent candidates. In Public Servant Councils elections, independent candidates had a considerable share (26.6%) in votes.

CHAPTER 5
Poland

Wieslawa Kozek, Michal Federowicz,
Witold Morawski

The first part of this chapter concentrates on property transformation, especially privatization. It is a controversial issue in Poland because it is linked, though not always justifiably, with declining standards of living and with unemployment of large sectors of the population. The second part discusses enterprise strategies and senior management behaviour against a background of increasing market forces. The final section discusses emerging patterns of relations, in terms of power and politics, between institutional actors at enterprise level, namely management, trade unions and employees' councils.[1]

The origin of property transformation and its forms in 1990–3

In the second half of the 1980s in Poland, discussions concerning different forms of enterprise ownership intensified. There were three basic themes in these debates, which favoured respectively traditional forms of privatization, continuing state ownership, and employee self-management. These approaches, which were then crystallizing, had a critical influence on the system emerging from the 1990 Privatization Act. By the autumn of 1990 arguments in favour of continuing state ownership were of less significance in the face of those pushing for privatization and employee self-management. The first of these, having strong government backing, favoured the classical model of privatization, based on the sale of enterprises, "case by case", through public offer. The second, enjoying popularity among employees and Solidarity activists, preferred self-government in enterprises and an increase in employee influence in property transformations.

The most classical type of privatization, despite a relatively small number of cases, is important, because it has had the most significant economic impact. This type of privatization is where equity shares are created which are then sold, but often with employees being offered them at preferential rates, the quantity of preferential shares for employees not exceeding 20 per cent of the total. In practice, employees have purchased less than 20 per cent of the total shares that have been made available to them. Firms that are privatized in this way are usually large, have a significant turnover and are more profitable. They are not only privatized through public offer but also through negotiations with large institutional investors, including foreign ones. Up to the time of writing, 86 enterprises have been privatized in this way.

Table 5.1 Number of transformed enterprises.

	1990	1991	1992	1993[a]	Total
Privatization by capitalization	6	24	22	34	86
Liquidation on the basis of the Privatization Act	44	372	299	130	845
Total	50	396	321	164	931
Liquidation on the basis of State Enterprise Act	28	506	319	258	1111
Commercialization[b]	52	226	150	–3	425
Total	80	732	469	255	1536
Total number privatized	130	1128	790	419	2467

Notes: (a) To the end of the third quarter; (b)After subtracting enterprises privatized by capitalization. Source: Data from the Central Statistical Office (GUS).

A form of property transformation specific to Poland is privatization by "liquidation". This is a rather misleading concept because it does not lead to the liquidation of the enterprise and because all legal and organizational changes are made without interrupting the enterprise's basic activities. The term comes from a special Act of 1988 which allows for the liquidation of state enterprises with the aim of privatizing them "experimentally". The practical conditions for such privatization were only established precisely in 1990, and the most common formula in this kind of privatization is "employee leasing". It is based on the concept that employees and external individuals can establish private companies and lease enterprise property from the state. This property is bought gradually from the state by the new company and, following the payment of all instalments, it becomes the property of the new company. The complete purchase of the enterprise takes place after a few years. However, from the start of its establishment, the new company manages the entire enterprise, and state agencies only exact payments, having no right to interfere in the management. The undertaking of this transformation is possible when it has been accepted by the employees. The consent of the employees' council, as well as that of the employee representatives' assembly is required (although once the company is transformed, both these agencies are liquidated). Additionally, the new company can be registered only when at least half of the employees have a stake in its ownership. The new shareholders must also raise capital which is equal in sum to one fifth of the book value of the enterprise property. External individuals may also have a stake in the new company and this usually occurs when employees do not have sufficient capital. But because this is a very convenient way to buy assets, financial institutions are not permitted to be shareholders. Despite legal guarantees, the name "employee-owned company" is misleading. Employees, as a collective, rarely have control over the company. Their shares are dispersed and, at the present time, there is no organizational form which represents their interests as shareholders. The controlling share is usually either in the hands of a small group of external shareholders or in the hands of management. In general, privatization by liquidation occurs mainly in small and middle-sized firms. Until now, 845 enterprises have been privatized in this manner. Privatization by capitalization and by liquidation on the basis of the 1990 Privatization Act leads, in almost all cases, to the authentic privatization of the enterprise. The liquidation of an enterprise is usually undertaken because of serious financial difficulties. This procedure differs from bankruptcy in that an effort is made to save the enterprise through the search for a purchaser of at least part of the enterprise.

Some large state enterprises are "commercialized" as a step to full privatization. Although formally transformed into companies, the state retains 100 per cent of the shares. This is usually a legal step towards the sale of state shares to private investors. In practice, however, of the 511 commercialized enterprises, private investors exist in only 86 cases. For the remaining "commercialized" enterprises, investors are either being approached or they will be asked to participate in the future Mass Privatization Programme. The change in legal status from "state enterprise" to "state treasury company" – that is, the commercialized companies – is important because employees' councils and employee representative assemblies are liquidated and, as in the majority of companies, boards of directors are elected by the owners. In the case of state treasury companies, two-thirds of the board of directors are appointed by the state authority (the Ministry of Property Transformations) and a third are nominated by employees. In practice, employees are usually represented on the boards of directors by middle-level management.

Summing up, close to 2,500 enterprises have undergone different forms of property transformation. Within this number, approximately 1,000 can be considered to be privatized, with the remainder either waiting to be privatized or being liquidated, and with their property assets being sold to private – usually small – owners.

It is possible to identify some general tendencies in the approach to the process of property transformation. Above all, the characteristic element of privatization in Poland, and probably also in other eastern and central European countries, is the extension of the concept of privatization to a very wide range of property transformations. There is, for example, a tendency to treat an enterprise as privatized even though most of its property remains in formal ownership of the state, although it is managed by a private company, as in the case of "employee leasing". A second characteristic of property transformation is that it is only one of many elements of change taking place in enterprises. Indeed, the transformation of property rights is not always the dominant element in the process whereby enterprises adapt to market conditions. There is the slow reorientation of companies, both state and privatized, according to the availability of resources. In general, privatization itself is more a context of market adaptations than a direct impulse. Most of the exceptions are the enterprises privatized by capitalization, when there is fundamental organizational restructuring. A third characteristic of property transformation is that the rules of privatization are not sufficiently binding or precise and the political context continues to be uncertain. Despite a continuation in the activities of state agencies, many essential issues have not been resolved and undergo continual modification. Examples of this are the regulations of the Leasing Acts affecting employee-owned companies, which can have a significant influence on the financial condition of these firms. Another example is the Enterprise Pact of 1992, the proposals of which may change decisively employee participation in property transformation. Further, continuous changes in prospects for mass privatization and the role of National Investment Funds results in uncertainties concerning the conditions of privatization. In the majority of state enterprises, final decisions on privatization have been suspended until more stable rules are put in place. A fourth characteristic of property transformation is the diversity of roles of the social actors in the enterprises. Trade unions and employees' councils were established originally in response to challenges different from those they face today. One can observe both "vindictive", but also more realistic, "policies" from the point of view of enterprises' future development. Similarly, enterprise management can behave in different ways – at times, it is conscious of its own interests, in which case it makes drastic internal changes. But on other occasions, it seems unable to prepare realistic plans for internal changes in enterprises and it remains a passive observer of a worsening situation. In general, the equilibrium of forces between different actors in the enterprises favours delays in privatization decisions. However, the non-symmetrical structure of forces between actors in state enterprise links processes of privatization to the interests of one of the partners of potential conflict in firms. This can lead to more rapid clarification of the privatization process and yet brutalize the internal relations of enterprises.

Among the four enterprises selected as case studies, each represents a different approach to privatization. In all of them, however, the perspective of property transformation has invoked strong reactions. The most advanced in the process of privatization is Medex. Before it was privatized, different possibilities were considered. In 1990-1, it searched for a foreign partner. This was later followed by "commercialization" and then by the quest for a domestic investor. Finally, an employee-owned company, without external capital, proved possible, primarily because of the favourable attitude of state bureaucrats because employees had raised sufficient capital. Important in the case of Medex is that the strong domination of management in all conflicts led to, at times, illegal activities and there is no doubt that the managing director was a main beneficiary of privatization. At the same time, internal changes carried out in the enterprise were undertaken in a dynamic and radical manner.

The case of enterprise Coldcuts is, in many ways, opposite to that of Medex and it is still a state-owned enterprise. In recent years, following a period of acute conflict between the employees' council and the man-

113

Table 5.2 Profile of the four industrial enterprises.

Enterprise dimensions	MEDEX	POLTOOLS	POWCOM	COLDCUTS
Branch	Medical equipment	Industrial tools	Electro-techniques	Food
Size: 1990	800	2,300	600	700
1994	200	1,300	300	670
Legal status	Stock company	State enterprise	One-person treasury company	State enterprise
Transformation method	Leasing	No change	No change	Leasing
Form of management	Management & supervisory board	Managerial contract	Management & supervisory board	Director & employment council
Profit/loss in past 2 years	Profit	Loss	Loss	Profit
Investment	Low	Low	None	Medium
Trade union (density)	Solidarity (10%)	Solidarity (ca.30%) OPZZ (ca.15%)	Solidarity (16%) OPZZ (18%)	Solidarity (13%) OPZZ (20%)
Trade union power	Weak	Strong	Weak	Strong
Managing director (last change)	1989	1993	1989	1981

aging director, a consensus was reached concerning the main objectives of the firm. The employees' council, which has strong support from Solidarity and is also trusted by employees, is generally in favour of privatization, although it does not wish to make such a decision "blindly". The managing director, while he would rather be the president of a private company than the director of a state-owned enterprise, is unable to act without the agreement of the employees' council, which prefers the employee-owned company as a model of privatization. The employees council understands this model to be a firm with a fairly even distribution of shares among employees. However, employees do not have sufficient capital for such a solution. Recently, the presence of a third actor, the Ministry of Property Transformation, has become more visible in the dealings of property transformations. The Ministry is using all possible means to persuade – it does not have the legal right to command – Coldcuts into the Mass Privatization Programme. It is worth noting that the Ministry is attempting to destroy the internal consensus within the enterprise, with the aim of weakening its resistance to joining the Mass Privatization Programme.

Powcom is a typical example of "commercialization". Initially, it sought a foreign partner. Then, because of a drastic worsening in its financial situation, it began "commercialization", partially as a response to promised tax relief, and partially in the hope of receiving aid from the Ministry in further searches for possible supplies of capital. None of these hopes, however, has brought the expected results. and at the same time, no force has emerged within the firm which is capable of putting forward a viable strategy.

Poltools offers an example of "mutual obstruction" by different forces within an enterprise. This is partly the result of bad experiences from quasi-privatization at the end of the 1980s. The then established "nomenclature companies", founded on ambiguous principles, led to internal conflicts among the personnel and a deep distrust of the management on the part of employees. Despite a few changes in management, later attempts to carry out necessary restructuring in the enterprise met with strong worker distrust. In this period, a battle for influence between the main actors of the enterprise – the management and Solidarity – dominated activities, while no real restructuring activities were carried out. But despite permanent financial difficulties, it has managed to maintain its competitiveness in the world market. Given this, its potential value is very high, although, paradoxically, internal consensus – essential if the firm is to pull out of a difficult situation – is difficult to attain. Restructuring attempts can easily lead to suspicions of what the majority see as an informal take-over of control of the enterprise by a small group of people motivated by their own material gains.

Among the four cases researched, we can speak of emerging strategies of adaptive changes in only two of them – Medex and Coldcuts. In Medex this is linked directly to privatization, whereas in Coldcuts, the strategies are not yet accompanied by property transformations. In this context, it is important to stress the unclear role of state agencies. Attempts to destroy the agreement between the management and the employees' council in Coldcuts have been pursued by Ministry bureaucrats because of their concern over the list of enterprises included in the

Mass Privatization Programme. Additionally, in the cases of Poltools and Powcom, government agencies are behaving passively, despite the fact that it is precisely they who hold the legal grounds for intervention. In both firms, a board of directors exists, two-thirds of whom are nominated by the Ministry. Both firms also have serious difficulties for which internal actors have been unable to work out resolution strategies. It appears that in such difficult situations, the representatives of state agencies do not bring long-term perspectives to a firm.

It is important to note a basic uncertainty concerning the character of the Mass Privatization Programme. The actual role of the the National Investment Funds has not yet been decided upon. In theory, they are to be controlled by the state only in the initial period. However, the influence of "coupon privatization" on the management of holdings could prove to be illusory. Rather than privatization, it could be yet one more version of state management, with neither the involvement of capital nor of employees. In opposition to the initial intentions behind the creation of the Mass Privatization Programme, a significant segment of the economy may be left permanently subject to state ownership through the National Investment Funds. Already, the political bargaining for control of these funds is visible.

Marketization as a context for the formation of industrial relations

The beginning of the 1990s in Poland was a period of turbulent change, the principal cause of which was the "Balcerowicz Plan". The plan was a government programme aimed at breaking the state protection of the economy; making enterprises function in a more realistic manner; withdrawing state subsidies; opening a national market for importers; and giving real value to the national currency. This created very difficult and previously unexperienced conditions for all economic enterprises, but it was to establish the foundation for the building of a market economy.

Many anticipated economic changes occurred and were accompanied by significant social costs. Reactions in response to the new situation varied: certain companies quickly began to adapt to competition, others did not. Above all, firms started to lose their former customers: they lost their former monopolistic position (as in the case of Powcom), the market in the former Soviet Union (the case of Poltools and Medex), and their large sales network (for example, Coldcuts). Furthermore, foreign producers entered the Polish market, offering similar products at lower prices (competitors for Poltools, Medex and Powcom) or new – initially smaller – and active domestic competitors emerged (Coldcuts). This meant the loss of former markets and, consequently, a respective decrease in orders, the necessity of limiting production, a drastic fall in the profitability rate, and consequential growing debt and need for reductions in employee numbers. The worst year in this respect was 1992. Enterprises were using 30–40 per cent of their production capacity and were reducing the number of employees, although the redundancy rate varied considerably.

The difficult economic situation created dissatisfaction among enterprises. Institutions of employee self-government and the Solidarity trade unions within the enterprises, channelled this dissatisfaction in the early period. Attempts to lessen the degree of dissatisfaction were directed towards the firm's general management. Competitions were announced and the positions were filled with people who were to be better managers, able to formulate more ambitious strategies and to be more in touch with the spirit of the new times. In three of the firms we researched, these changes occurred. In the fourth, the former general manager maintained his position because of his past active opposition to the larger conglomerate organizational structures – *kombinat*. On a broader scale, the sphere of personnel changes is illustrated by research conducted on a representative sample in the Mazovia region (within a 150 km radius of Warsaw), which showed that 20 per cent of the general managers were replaced (Kozek 1991). The selection of a new general manager, however, did not always give immediate results. To a large degree, this depended on how far the new managers recognized that changes on the macro scale would be continued. The acceptance of the assumption that macro changes are irrevocable resulted in attempts to work out a recovery strategy. The failure by top management to accept this inevitably resulted in a period of waiting for state intervention.

The loss of market outlets through the reduction of production forced the management of firms to reduce staff numbers. This has had a significant influence on the actors in industrial relations. In the initial period of reform, trade unions and employees' councils easily accepted serious reductions in personnel. In all the firms researched, redundancies have occurred. They took a drastic form in Powcom,

Medex and Poltools. In the Polish industrial system, employee organizations have the right to be informed of planned reductions. The enterprise management may consult the employees about its decision but need not take their opinions into account. However, protests against such decisions occurred only rarely. This phenomenon is confirmed in the enterprises: protests against reductions never occurred, with employees recognizing the necessity of lay-offs.

Furthermore, the recession has caused a significant drop in the real value of earnings. Wages have increased systematically (in terms of US dollars),[2] but at the same time a rapid rise in the price of goods and services has made it difficult for families to satisfy their needs. In only one of the case studies were protests from employees' organizations more expressive: Poltools organized a strike alert. Restructuring problems, however, have proved to be more important causes of debate within enterprises.

The main trade unions of the Polish industrial system

OPZZ and Solidarity, in the initial period of transformation, presented themselves as pro-reform. In connection with this, Solidarity itself claimed to create a protective umbrella for the consecutive governments. OPZZ instead strove towards greater independence. Neither of them, however, undertook any serious protest action which could be considered a confrontation with the government. Both Solidarity and OPZZ organized, on average, one day of strike alerts annually. Many employees tried to be exempt from participating in the strike alert. This was the case in Coldcuts and Poltools, which received permission from the regional trade union authorities. In exchange, meetings were organized or flags were hung.

This does not at all mean that in the Polish industrial system there is no tendency to strike. Strikes have occurred in firms on the verge of bankruptcy, in large plants and in those for which no recovery programme has been found. In firms where there are no signs of bankruptcy – Coldcuts, Powcom and Poltools – the management has worked out restructuring plans that provide a certain measure of job security.

The recession has also encouraged the phenomenon of the divisionalization of large economic units into smaller subunits. Multi-plant enterprises have divided. It was considered that a smaller firm would function more easily in the market. Furthermore, it was believed that it would be easier to rationalize the costs of production in smaller firms because it would be easier to know these costs. On the other hand, this tendency was favoured by many employees' councils, trade unions and personnel who wanted to work "on their own". In the firms under study, the tendencies to separate the parts from the whole, and eliminate branches and regional divisions, have occurred: Coldcuts separated from a large multi-plant enterprise; Powcom eliminated its less profitable and technologically independent regional branch, which was apportioned (for capital) to another company; Medex has separated into smaller parts; and Poltools has loosened economic ties with its branches, part of its capital being apportioned to many private companies. The other effect of the recession has been a drop in the profitability of the firms, and many of them lost their capacity for financing. Additionally, some were forced to accept credits, at an interest rate of 40 per cent or more per year, not for investments but for turnover – this situation occurred in Poltools. In Medex, Coldcuts and Powcom the debt trap has been avoided, though each of them has faced the problem of unrecoverable debts from their customers.

Planning for the future of the firm, its development and restructuring without access to financial means is often impossible, thereby making the management situation critical. Management is, in most cases, unable to put forth a programme of radical changes. All changes concerning different products are especially hampered because of the need for technological changes. Only two of the firms, Medex and Coldcuts, have been able to finance small investments from their own resources. This inability to make radical change significantly weakened management because only a strong partner with vision would have been trusted. In most cases, at least initially, management has been structurally weak. In the period between 1988 and 1993, the conception of the "Bermuda triangle" (a term that became established in Poland in the 1980s) was confirmed. It meant that the state enterprise was ruled by the triad of management, trade unions and employees' council. Every decision or programme, regardless of its reasonableness, once in the triangular structure became inefficient, contextual and unfocused. In 1993 the recession came to an end with a tendency for the level of production to cease declining.[3] Employee lay-offs also stopped and profitability rates improved. In industrial relations, an immediate strengthening of management's position was a result, and it is now rare that new vacancies for positions of general manager are announced. Why did employees and their organizations not act in defence of the real value of their wages and salaries, and other essential problems concerning working conditions? An important reason was the dominant conviction that an improvement in the quality of life would be achieved through privatization. However, a conviction that the state enterprise cannot be reformed prevents people from seeing alternatives to privatization. There are many examples of this in our study. In Coldcuts, the belief that state ownership is only transitory is dominant: employees, trade unions and employees' councils are counting on the possibility of a significant pay rise in relation to the lessening of tax burdens following the privatization decision. A similar attitude is common in Powcom: it is considered that the final privatization of the firm will allow for an increase in wages and salaries. In Poltools, the possibility of a change in the level of pay under existing conditions is not considered. In Medex, the one privatized firm which was studied, wages have increased slightly.

Enterprise strategies and the role of management

In the initial period of the transformation the contention that state enterprises did not develop active strategies in response to macroeconomic changes – made as a result of the implementation of the principles of the "Balcerowicz Plan" – was widespread. With time, it became clear that only a small number of the state firms had developed these programmes. Other enterprises started adaptive activities and a small number of firms did not respond at all, adopting a strategy of so-called "waiting". Kozek, carrying out research on the strategies of 100 state and private firms in the Mazovia region, estimated that 40 per cent of the firms have made no adjustments, 26 per cent have rationalized their activities internally, and only 21 per cent have adjusted to the market in an active and aggressive manner (Kozek 1992). It is important to appreciate, therefore, the fact that each of our four case study firms developed and implemented adjustment strategies.

Coldcuts This middle-sized enterprise in the meat industry has implemented a marketization plan. It is based on the active search for

120

customers for its products, the introduction of a variety of new products, and investment in machinery and equipment which made the change of production possible. To cut back on production costs, less expensive suppliers of raw materials have been sought, in both domestic and foreign markets. The firm has not taken any bank credits and it has realized a plan of employment reduction through a strategy of retirements, etc. In the company's management declaration, the concern is with maintaining market position through the supply of good quality products and fast reactions to customer orders. The plans are always focused on the short-term – one year at the most. This is because of the annual financial accounting, which details what percentage of profits can be converted into investments. Management try to use the money wisely and all decisions are made after many internal consultations. Following an initial period, in which the firm was free to make decisions and attained relative success, it has decided to wait for macro-political decisions concerning the conditions of privatization. It has been resting on its laurels, satisfied with the fact that it has not lost its market position. The decisions on privatization, however, have not been forthcoming. In this situation a gradual change was made in the strategy of action in the firm: because of the privatization plans of the enterprise by leasing its assets from the state its market expansion has been curbed significantly and attempts to attain high profitability rates were abandoned. This was done because such a strategy would lead to an increase in its market value which was not in line with what the main actors in the enterprise wanted. For the management of the firm, and both trade unions and employees' council, the strategic aim consists of maintaining the firm's value at the lowest price possible, in conditions of social harmony.

The formulation of strategies in Coldcuts and its changes have occurred through the co-operative efforts of the main actors of the firm who, following a period of researching their own mutual possibilities and a short period of conflict, began to work closely together. The management of the firm is undoubtedly the motor of change. The firm is directed by a middle-aged engineer who is wise, thrifty and identifies with the firm. His social origin is rural, and this is accompanied by all the positive attitudes of a Polish farmer towards work and running things efficiently. He is diligent, works hard, and is fair and calculating. He has inculcated his farmer-specific approach into the group of top management working with him. They too are mainly engineers interested in the technological aspects of their work and, through trial and error, test their economic intuitions on the market. This group would like to guide the firm through the difficult period without "losing face". They are mainly concerned with maintaining jobs for both management and the rest of the personnel. However, management does not possess competence in human relations, and it is incessantly in conflict with the employees' council which, in fact, shares similar aims.

Medex   This small medical equipment producer, led by a new management group (selected on the basis of competition), faced the problem of foreign competition and a sharp reduction in domestic and foreign markets, (because of the breakdown of the Soviet market and its dependent countries). In this situation, management has forced the firm to accept a drastic cutback in all costs regardless of the strain on the personnel. Production has been limited and specialized, employment reduced and the unproductive properties of the firm have been sold. Investment decisions are made cautiously and in very specific areas. Senior management aims at holding on to the most valuable assets of the firm, with the hope that they will at some time take them over. The role of trade unions and employees' councils in this case is marginal. The general manager is not emotionally committed to the staff and he is therefore guided primarily by his own interest. The strategy is characterized as a fight for survival at all costs. The aim of concentrating on the market and eliminating all that seemed unnecessary (people, assets, etc.) under the new situation, has been relatively successful. The firm has a chance of surviving as long as it can convince its customers that it is a solid producer.

Poltools   This industrial machinery enterprise – relatively large for Polish conditions – collapsed in 1992 because of the loss of a product market and work co-ordination problems. Subsequently, the four top management bodies were unable to work out a cohesive plan for restructuring that would be acceptable to trade unions. These bodies aimed at sectioning off portions for themselves in newly established companies. In 1992 it appeared that other companies, already privatized, had succeeded in paralysing the market for the firm's products. The new management under-estimated the durability of macro-structural change and expected some kind of state protection over the firm, given the political bargaining force of the workers who were among the most active in the country. The consecutive restructuring plans needed to take into account realistically the strength of the informal structures in Poltools and in the companies it generated. However, the trade unions, in particular Solidarity, did not agree to these plans: Solidarity announced its readiness to strike, despite lack of support from the regional structure. Finally, the company succeeded in changing some top management personnel, although the trade union this time had to redefine the aims of the strike to conform to the legislation. The union's strength became apparent because its position was acknowledged by the Ministry of Ownership Transformations. However, the power of the union appeared as a negative force. Not one constructive proposal was put forward by the union because it had no members competent to do so, nor did it have enough support from either the regional or the national structure. Consecutive managements tried to clarify the organizational structures by determining the ownership form, but this did not reduce its internal problems. The result has been a lack of a market strategy, a failure to acquire new customers and markets, and a lack of resolve to lower expenses significantly or to improve the quality of production. The competence of the succeeding managements has varied, but none of them were capable of developing new ideas for the future of the firm. The so-called "bad debts" limited management manoeuvrability significantly. The firm has now been forced to seek bank credits and is constantly threatened with a bank refusal and therefore bankruptcy. Senior management is faced with a very short-term perspective: literally from week to week. The problems of the firm are too overwhelming for the capabilities of the average Polish manager.

Powcom This company specializes in powder metallurgy and developed an active adjustment strategy in the initial period. It cut itself off from a technologically independent and almost loss-making regional division. It did not have market losses immediately (it had a monopoly on the domestic market without the right to export). The firm's domestic market closed down very slowly. For this reason, the firm continued to be profitable in the initial period. Accompanied by a feeling of financial success, it strove for rapid property transformation. The employees' council and trade unions supported senior management's plan to transform it into a one-person State Treasury company. This plan was carried out efficiently. Shortly after this, the domestic market crashed because of the lowering of duty barriers on final products and component parts. The result was a drastic lowering in production: from large serial production it had to change to small serial production and often undertook the development of prototypes and even unitary products. Lay-offs became necessary. Senior management carried out a strategy of gradual change in order not to alarm the section of personnel that was decisive in maintaining the basic production capacity. The remaining employees, less qualified and less useful, were eliminated gradually, fired, or were forced to leave through a policy of low pay. The main aim of the top management was to resolve payments with the State Treasury so that the state structures would have no reason to intervene in the functioning of the company. The aim of this strategy was to wait for the right moment to privatize. The top management undoubtedly had been counting on taking over many of the company's shares, though this plan was illusory. The main weakness in the strategy undertaken by top management has been an inability to adjust the techniques of management to the changing conditions dictated by the changes in the scale of production. Too much time has been spent determining how to change the organizational structure of the firm, as well as in deciding how to adapt the style of managing production teams to the new requirements connected with the work on prototypes. The general characteristic of the firm's strategy is caution and waiting, and this is probably a consequence of its analysis of the government's privatization strategy. An additional factor is that the firm is managed by a group of older managers with a lot of work experience, who are constantly in doubt as to whether or not the new private owner will use their services properly. Consequently, they favour the continuation of the present situation, where nothing is yet decided.

In conclusion, we can say that the researched cases illustrate the variability of enterprise adaptation to new economic situations and new systemic solutions. The question of why some of these companies carried out these adjustments, others did so to a lesser degree, and some not at all, is interesting. The first factor which should be pointed out is that adjustments would not be possible at all if the rest of society did not allow for the initiation and continuation of market reforms and ownership transformations. As a result, industrial relations have developed relatively peacefully. Social protests against the costs of the changes have been much more subdued than either the political elite or theoreticians of change expected. The researched cases illustrate that rather than being a field of particularly acute conflict, the enterprise may offer a space of co-operation for the sake of a better future. The second factor can be interpreted in terms of action theory. It is clear that individuals and social groups read the meaning of present activities by referring to past experiences, and these activities are constituted through the perspective of influencing the future. In some companies, active adaptation was impossible because of particular past experiences. These were experiences which caused the management to misunderstand the necessity of radical adaptation to the market, nor did they acknowledge that the government was ready to agree to the destruction of the productive property of companies if they ceased to be profitable under the new conditions. Past experience has also often prevented management from taking risks: that is, to balance the costs and the profits, to demonstrate a capacity in the field of marketing, the analysis of cost structures, and the management of employees. In most cases, experience has proved to be an obstacle. This applies to both management and trade union activists because, in general, a belief in the necessity of market reforms has not been linked with practical recognition of methods by which they can be realized. Trade unionists tend not to believe that the social cost of changes will be high, and they rely on the supportive function of the state: social security, for example. The factor which, conversely, had a positive influence on the formulation of active strategies of adaptation is the vision of the future, and within this perspective, the constellation of current interests. If a company's management perceives the possibility of approval for a new strategy through some sector of staff, it often decides to keep the enterprise viable and take it over from the State Treasury. This game, for example, was played by the Medex management. Recognition of the possibility that the strategy of a firm can be effective is decisive in determining whether the firm's attempts to survive in the market becomes achievable. The degree to which a company's management feels committed to its staff and obliged to defend their interests and jobs also influences the character of strategy and the costs of its realization. When management–personnel links are weak, the possibilities of bolder proposals for solutions and greater rationalization of activities in relation to the dictates of the market become more plausible. In the case of strong manager–worker relations, the tendency for defensive strategies emerges, which after some time can prove to be ineffective and delay the implementation of necessary changes.

Institutional actors in action: between power and politics

Co-operation is implicit in industrial organization, because those who choose to be employed accept the nature of their contract. This appears to be the nature of utilitarian forms of organization (Etzioni 1961). In reality, however, the situation is more complex because industrial organizations are often two-sided, like the Roman deity Janus with two faces: with one turned towards co-operation and the other towards conflict (Bendix 1956). The formation of a stable composition of elements of co-operation and conflict – the industrial relations system – requires a stabilization of the rules of the game between actors. But it is difficult to attain this state in conditions of systemic change, as has happened in Poland. Hence, in the fifth year of changes, the rules of the game are changing constantly. In brief, the process of stabilization is far from complete (Morawski 1993). An explanation of the causes of this situation is made difficult by the fact that there are many different factors involved: purely economic (for example, the lack of a product market for enterprise production); economic and political (for example, privatization, which is a process inspired both from above and from below); political (for example, the politicization of trade unions, and legislative changes); and social (for example, the character of the workforce and its political involvement). In this situation, one can only show how different and how variable industrial relations are in the process of transformation. This is why, on the basis of the four case studies, we shall describe some emerging elements in patterns of industrial relations.

In Medex the most important actor in this medical equipment enterprise is the general manager. He is a ruthless man when it comes to realizing set goals. He assumed his position in June 1989, after winning the competition for the position of general manager. Prior to this, he had been a youth activist, a so-called *"apparatchik"*. He has many informal connections. The trade unions are his main partners. "Solidarity", however, is not a very active trade union. Approximately a quarter of the employees are members of Solidarity. It is worth noting that it uses the legal advice of the union's regional headquarters. The other, formerly larger, trade union, OPZZ, no longer exists. In practice, the power of trade unions is virtually non-existent. We should also mention the employees' council, which initiated a change of the general manager in January 1988. At that time, this was an act of courage. Now the council no longer exists. The employees are characterized by a lack of aspiration to participate in the decision-making process. They are clearly disorganized and ambivalent. The general manager is fighting successfully for the survival of the enterprise in the turbulent market. He acts in the belief that employees' organizations are obstacles to the realization of his adaptive strategy. This is why he marginalized the influence of Solidarity. He also eliminated OPZZ trade union activists brutally by firing two of its main activists illegally (the labour court ruled in favour of the activists). He saw no need to consult the employees' council. For a long time, he did not call a council meeting because he wanted first to complete the process of decision-making concerning privatization. The two general managers today own the controlling interest of the enterprise. Both the trade unions and the employees' council (self-government) strongly indicated that they acted in the interests of the employees. They did not, however, have sufficient professional knowledge or experience in socio-political activities to formulate and realize an alternative to the general manager's solution. This explains why they did not have the opportunity to become equal partners with the general manager. The employees were passive, as they were inclined to conform to governmental policy while accepting the propaganda of the mass media that there was no other alternative, in the form of activities, to be adopted within the enterprise. In reciprocal relations between the general manager and the trade unions, we are dealing with a situation in which the trade unions are not permitted – because of the cunning of the general manager – to develop any activity which might be antagonistic towards the general manager. One manifestation of the cunning of the general manager was his decision to demonstrate his strength by eliminating the trade union OPZZ rather than Solidarity. One can suppose that in different circumstances, his victim might have been Solidarity. It can be assumed that the general manager does not only want to keep the process of decision-making from being social, he is also not ready to tolerate any control by the workers. The general manager is not only using his professional knowledge and connections, but, above all, the leverage over the workers given by the threatening situation the enterprise faces, which has been created by the impact of the government's macroeconomic policy. This policy has caused the threatened employees to focus on keeping their jobs. They are therefore prepared to agree to the solutions put forward by the general manager, privatization included, which is more profitable to the general manager than to the employees.

In Medex, the general manager is the driving force leading the enterprise to better economic conditions and choosing the option of "privatization through liquidation". The enterprise is now expanding its activities and may be considered to have a strategy already formulated. This could be evaluated positively, especially in contrast to situations in other enterprises. It is precisely these factors that lead many people in this enterprise to describe the role of the general manager as "creative". The issue that is of most interest, however, is that of the elimination of other social actors: the liquidation of the trade union OPZZ, the elimination of the employees' council, the weakening of Solidarity, the intimidation of personnel, etc. The emergence of these actors in the 1980s was one of the conditions of systemic change. Yet in Medex the general manager's power is now clearly visible. He unilaterally imposes his solutions on both the institutional partners and employees. The employees of Medex once again find themselves incapacitated, without either articulation or representation of their interests and values. Has Medex regressed to the "pre–Solidarity" era, then, when it established itself as an independent enterprise, or to the era, to use a Western comparison, of the Taylorist form of organization? The response to the above question is twofold. The doubts are expressed by the social democrats. For them, Medex represents so-called "free capitalism", and not capitalism "with a human face", which they are eager to accept. The neo-liberals do not share these anxieties, however. They believe that what has occurred in the enterprise is necessary because it is now easier to focus on economic efficiency. At most, they regret that the enterprise has become an employee-owned company, which they consider to be only a transitory form. For them, privatization is for the common good, even at the cost of marginalizing social actors and eliminating employees.

At Poltools, in the 1980s, underground Solidarity was a powerful force. It remains strong and active (with approximately 450 members). Solidarity is visible not only on the enterprise level as a whole, but also in its divisions where its representatives consult workers on wage systems and other decisions. Solidarity retains a worker's character, which makes it different from OPZZ, which gathers many people from management. Currently, the employees' council is not at all active in the enterprise, although it is still a state-owned enterprise, and no one seems to be interested in its revival. General managers have changed often in recent years. In January 1992, with the help of Solidarity and the employees' council, a supervisor (who had formerly been the deputy director for labour relations) was appointed to the enterprise (as a general manager) by the Ministry. This was the first so-called managerial contract in Poland. He was an ambitious person, with a rather adversarial disposition towards employee organizations. The experiment failed and, after eighteen months, he was recalled. Relations are bad between the present general manager and employees' organizations; the latter had counted clearly on being invited to participate in the major restructuring of economic, production and social policies. The premise by which they were guided was simple: they wanted to control the decisions because they were afraid that "the enterprise would be pilfered". The general manager promised Solidarity that it would be consulted on decisions; however, he has not kept his word. For example, he refused to show the trade unions the project for restructuring. He wanted the trade unions to be concerned exclusively with issues of working conditions and pay, not of the entire enterprise. He did not want to transfer the social property to a special foundation, although this transfer was supported by Solidarity. Solidarity has thus become less flexible: now each time the general manager announces a change, Solidarity announces a strike alert. Conflict between the two trade unions is also present, and the general manager tries to play the unions off against each other.

The main result is a stalemate of socially active forces in the enterprise. As well organized and experienced forces, they are capable of using resources such as formal rights, competence, tradition, informal structures, etc. It is enough to block the carrying out of imposed change, that the general manager would like to implement. The only clear thing about his conception of the situation, is that he wants to do it alone. The alternative to imposed change is negotiated change, which is believed to be a better option (Crozier & Friedberg 1977). But negotiated change has not yet made it here. The negotiation mechanisms can also lead to the blocking of change, even in conditions of the high culture of negotiations (Wildavsky & Pressman 1974). In Poltools, it is clear that negotiated change is desired. There is not, however, the compulsion for negotiation through which mutual exchanges would be made – between the interested sides – via trade-offs. This could be explained partially by the relatively good economic performance of the enterprise. This is why there is no immediate need to find a solution. It would probably be easier to implement changes were the social forces from below (i.e. Solidarity, OPZZ, employees) weaker. This is exactly what the general manager had in mind. He failed, however, and as a result has recently been dismissed.

In Powcom, the general manager, like the rest of the managerial staff, has been employed in the enterprise since the start of his professional career. He attained his position after being selected for the post in 1990. He is an engineer and a rather indecisive person. There are two trade unions in Powcom, and neither has many members. Solidarity has twice as many members as OPZZ (25 per cent of the employees in total) and is a more active and influential trade union. The trade unions co-operate with one another, which is common at enterprise level, but not at national level. The employees' council which was active in the past, was liquidated when the enterprise was transformed into a one-person State Treasury company. The number of employees continues to decrease (a fall from approximately 600 to about 300), with salaries among the lowest, although highly qualified employees are still well paid.

Trade unions are at present interested almost exclusively in pay, working conditions, some production issues and the training of the managerial staff. The strategic issues in which Solidarity was interested two or three years ago are now beyond its range of interests. Solidarity came to the conclusion (as did OPZZ) that its ambition could not be too high at the present time. This means that, in principle, they are not disposed to any confrontation. Solidarity, however, has made a few moves which do have this character. It called the general manager for talks with women employees earning the lowest incomes; wrote a petition to the general manager; and it initiated the writing of an article in a newspaper which revealed the high income of the general manager; but it does not initiate strikes, because employees are opposed to them. Solidarity is constantly losing prestige and its representative lost in the elections for the board of directors. The board of directors even finds it acceptable not to inform Solidarity about its main decisions. Trade unions are losing their importance, it appears. In this situation, the enterprise is not only the victim of its own relative technological and organizational backwardness, and the incompetence of management, etc., but also of external factors which are not conducive to overcoming these legacies of the past. This causes the trade unions to back out of areas where they were formerly active. At present, they are limited to, at most, a consultive function or occasional contesting of decisions concerning work conditions and pay.

Coldcuts is managed successfully by a middle-aged engineer with a calculating mentality, who works with a group of other engineers. Loyalty is more important than competence in Coldcuts. Two trade unions are active in the enterprise. The branch trade union is more numerous (140 members) than is Solidarity (90 members). Solidarity gathers workers with slightly higher qualifications and is more influential than the branch union. There is a clear rivalry between the two unions for new members, and in their programmes and methods of realization. For example, the branch union has for a long time, and consistently, supported privatization, whereas Solidarity was, and is, distrustful of the successive proposals for property transformation. There is, however, no open conflict between them. In Coldcuts, as in every state enterprise, there is an employees' council. The general manager has to take into account the views of the council because it has the right to fire him and appoint a new general manager. This is possible because the state relinquished control over personnel policies in the enterprise. The general manager consults the employees' council on all important decisions concerning the enterprise. The council, on the other hand, co-operates closely with "Solidarity". A coalition of these two institutions is capable of blocking the decisions of the general manager. However, it is unable to force him to make any serious decisions concerning the modernization of the enterprise, nor is it able to break up the "family" and "clique" make-up which governs Coldcuts or is capable of changing the system of payment. It does not, however, go further than the exercising of what is called "negative power". In general, employees, Solidarity and the employees' council want a type of privatization over which they would have control. In practice, this means support for employee-owned companies, which are very popular in Poland (Jarosz 1994). Other solutions raise doubts: for example, the recent idea of the general manager to sell a majority of shares to a Swiss–Polish firm (which would solve the financial problems of the enterprise). The council and Solidarity prefer equal shares for the employees without a strong foreign contracting party, but were they to recognize the necessity of a strategic investor, they would still prefer a Polish company.

From the four case studies we can conclude as follows. First, the constitution of an actor, even, it would seem, one as embedded as Solidarity itself, or popular among the personnel as are employees' councils, does not yet mean that in conditions of Polish systemic transformation this actor's existence is guaranteed, especially in small and medium-sized enterprises. As we know, in many such enterprises, especially private ones, there are no trade unions at all. This shows that one of the functional requirements of mature industrial relations is not fulfilled, namely, the emergence of a strong, organized workforce, because only such a body will articulate and represent its interests well. The situation is much better in large enterprises and strong industrial branches such as mining, the shipping industry and defence. Secondly, that reciprocal relations between industrial partners are not relations of mutual respect and trust, but rather of suspicion, rivalry and hostility. They aim not at organized present and future co-operation, but at undermining one another's position, perhaps even eliminating it. This does not only result from the weakness of the actors, but from the external context as well: the situation of the enterprise on the market, willingness toward ownership transformation, and the strong politicization of the trade union movement on the national level. Thirdly, that there is no refined culture of negotiation. It appears that mutual agreements are only temporary settlements which can be changed according to the situation, whereas the mature enterprise is a negotiating system between various social forces that know they will be around for a long time and recognize one another. Because this situation has not yet emerged, it means that industrial relations are not yet consolidated, and that the rules of the game might be changed. It appears that the game in the enterprise could be a zero sum game which means that power relations are at stake, whereas the establishment of the system of industrial relations promises politics: that is, a positive sum game. Finally, that institutions of industrial democracy are, however, generally capable of ensuring negative power for themselves. This is enough to stop a decision by management which would be even less favourable to the personnel. However, this to has its own negative consequences, namely that enterprise development is then stalled. It cannot therefore actively adapt to changing market conditions; in other words, it cannot become a fully economically-efficient enterprise. The delay of the institutionalization of industrial relations therefore delays the structural transformation of the entire economy.

Conclusions

The case studies illustrate the main tendencies in industrial relations in the period of systemic change in Poland. They suggest that Solidarity, the main force behind the initial period of systemic change, did not at first step back from taking responsibility for adaptive programmes at the level of industrial enterprises (Pankow 1993). At the national level, this was expressed in the form of a "protective umbrella" for consecutive governments. It was also expressed in the collective behaviour and preferences of the workers, the modal pattern of which Gardawski (1992) describes as "moderate modernization". That is, the workers support the market order but they modify it such that in this order, there will "be a place for them". At the level of the enterprises we investigated, this protective attitude found its expression in the "umbrella" extended by all trade unions (Solidarity, OPZZ and employees' councils) over the adaptive programmes undertaken by various managements: for example, the acceptance of lay-offs, lower salaries and wages, and restraint from striking. The case studies also indicate that the realization of market and privatization programmes led to the emergence of different group interests. It appears that there are some who gain and others who lose in the process of the realization of the programme. Our cases illustrate that among the winners are management – managing directors in particular – while the losers are less-skilled employees and, often, their representatives – trade unions and employees' councils.

One may suggest that the institutions of employees' representatives, since they are focused on defensive activities, do not at present represent a strong force for transformation. The transformation suffers because it could be more easily achieved with the help of group interests from below. Our case studies prove that both the employees' councils and Solidarity, and to a lesser degree OPZZ trade unions, are able to develop projects offering constructive solutions, but at the same time, these projects are not as developed professionally as those from management. But even though they are less mature, they have the legitimizing quality of a system of industrial relations. For the enterprise management, however, this does not seem to be important. It must be stressed that ownership changes are not the only, and often not even the main, element of gradual restructuring in enterprises which are undergoing this process. Restructuring, although it is proceeding slowly, encompasses all functioning spheres of the company, such as recruitment, the wage system, management of the firm and its finances, the organizational structure, limited technological modernization, and market policies. In state owned enterprises, however, which are not undergoing ownership changes, essential market adjustments are also being carried out. In these enterprises, the perspective of ownership transformation is a very important element influencing relations between actors within the company. Even if the real possibility for privatization appears unclear for the future, the struggle for control over enterprise resources has already begun.

As we said earlier, there is a direct influence of ownership transformations on industrial relations at the enterprise level. It is based on strengthening the position of management while at the same time diminishing the role of employee representation. The weakening of employee influence on management shows first in the liquidation of employee councils, and secondly in the often considerable weakening of trade unions. The legal role of trade unions is the same in every company, regardless of the kind of ownership. In state-owned enterprises, however, trade unions have a greater ability to go beyond the established competence level: for example, through influencing the composition of employee councils. At the same time it should be stressed that the legal competence of employee councils (according to the 1981 legislation), which have not been hindered by informal limitation of a political nature since 1989, are unusually broad. Of course, the actual influence of employees councils on management is very variable, but in general privatization is a chance for management to minimize the influence of employees (Federowicz 1992).

Finally, changes linked with adaptation to the market economy, as well as ownership changes, should be perceived as elements of institutional change. Changes in economic mechanisms, legal institutions and broadly understood social institutions were the essence of transformation. In particular, bargaining about the manner of ownership transformation began a series of negotiations between various actors on two levels: the national and the enterprise. On the national level, it appeared to be strongest in the period of debates over privatization legislation (passed by Parliament in July 1990), and then in the period of negotiations connected with the "Enterprise Pact" (between the government and trade unions, with the participation of employers' organizations) and later with its implementation. One part of the Pact concerns the supplementation of previous methods of ownership transformations. It could be assumed that until the privatization process is exhausted, from time to time the need of revision of its detailed principles will return and it will provoke a further series of negotiations at the national level. At the same time, the realization of the Enterprise Pact means the implementation of a corporatist solution. At the level of the enterprise, preparing itself for ownership transformation, concrete changes are always preceded by a period of uncertainty among actors inside the company concerning possible gains and losses. A legal and authentically respected condition of initiating ownership transformation is the attainment of consensus within the enterprise which accepts the change. This gives rise to tension and often conflicts. It is impossible to bring about transformation in ownership, however, if these conflicts are not resolved.

Notes

1. The section on property transformation was written by M. Federowicz; the discussion of enterprise strategies is by W. Kozek; and the final section was written by W. Morawski.
2. For an hour of work in 1993, an industrial Polish worker was paid 1.4 USD. *Rzeczpospolita*, n.15 (3664), 19 January 1994, p. 7.
3. The growth in industrial production in 1993 was 7.4 per cent. *Economy and market*, n.15 (3664) 19 January 1994.

CHAPTER 6
Russia

Vladimir Gerchikov

Introduction

The process of economic reform in Russia, in relation to the operation of enterprises, has gone through a number of stages. In 1987 legal changes allowed enterprises to operate free from ministry controls and with the ability to establish their own links with suppliers and customers. However, it is indicative of the traditional patterns of enterprise management that they did not immediately seize these opportunities. An important stimulus to managerial autonomy in relation to the internal structures of enterprises came with the 1989 law on co-operatives, which gave management autonomy to create co-operatives within their own organizations. These operated outside ministerial controls on wages and the tax regime for enterprises. The first permissive regulation at the end of the 1980s relating to the ownership of enterprises was concerned with the leasing (*arenda*) of enterprises from the ministries; this gave enterprises freedom to reform their internal structures.[1]

The main changes in normative regulations affecting enterprises occurred as recently as 1992 under the Yeltsin Government. These took two main forms: macroeconomic price and wage liberalization, and ownership change. The initial programme of privatization was published in June 1992 and was confined to the service and construction sectors, but three weeks later it was decreed that enterprises in most industries were to be transformed into joint-stock companies. There was then a rapid succession of decrees on ownership change, which created confusion for enterprise managers.

137

This chapter discusses some of these processes of reform and their implications for labour relations, with reference to data collected from enterprises in the Novosibirsk region of Russia. Although these enterprises have a number of specific features, as discussed below, the changes within them are indicative of broader processes, not only within the Novosibirsk region, but in the country as a whole.

The case study enterprises

The main content of this chapter is the analysis of contemporary labour relations in industrial enterprises in the process of transition from the command to the market economy. The results of our[2] research showed that the most important influences on the labour relations system were rendered by: the privatization of state and municipal property; changes in the general economic situation in the country and in enterprises' business and production strategy; restructuring and the development of financial relations inside enterprises; a high inflation rate; and a fall in employees' real income.

This chapter is based mainly on data that was collected by in-depth investigation of four enterprises situated in the regional capitals of Novosibirsk and Krasnoyarsk (See Table 6.1). There were three stages of research at each enterprise in 1992–3. At each stage enterprise statistics and documents were analyzed and detailed interviews (each of 1–2 hours) were carried out with 20–40 representatives of the different

Table 6.1   Case study enterprises.

Enterprise	Branch of industry	Product	Number of employees at beginning of 1992	at end of 1993
First sample				
SIBERTURB	Engineering	Large electric machines	3200	2600
LEBAGS	Light industry	Leather haberdashery	800	780
ELMACH	Metallurgy	Metal rolling	8500	6200
MATOOLS	Engineering	Machine tools	850	1000
Second sample				
ALMETAL	Metallurgy	Aluminium ingots	11600	13000
AERO	Air Transport	Transport	2500	2000
FOUNDRY	Engineering	Foundry equipment	2300	1600

groups of employees, management, trade unions and other, voluntary, organizations such as enterprise councils and employee partnerships. Further research was carried out at three other enterprises, and we also refer to data from these in this discussion. Publications and materials of two regional trade union associations were also used.

Before considering labour relations at enterprise level it is necessary to situate changes in their wider political and economic context, and it is to this we turn first.

Privatization – national strategy

The state privatization programme announced on 11 June 1992 proclaimed as its main aims the following tasks: to form a stratum of private property owners who will support the development of a socially orientated market economy; to increase the efficiency of enterprises and to provide for the social protection of the population.[3] The main areas of privatization were to be enterprises in the electricity, food, construction and building materials industries, and in sectors providing technical support for agriculture, transport, trade, public catering and social services. However, three weeks later (on 1 July 1992), the President's decree[4] was issued on the subject of accelerating the transformation of enterprises in the majority of industries into joint-stock companies of the open type.[5] The decree specified the transformation procedure including standard articles for the joint-stock company[6]. This decree encouraged many enterprises to start privatization programmes, although they had not prepared plans for this. Thus, one of the case studies Siberturb, which had been a leased enterprise since 1 August 1990, increased its own capital gradually and bought parts of the leased assets, aiming to buy them up completely by 1995–6. In the middle of 1992, the enterprise suffered a severe shortage of working capital (because of "price liberalization") and had no funds available to buy the remaining assets. Being afraid that the state might worsen the conditions of privatization and deprive the enterprises of the advantages proclaimed in the legislation, the management of this company, with the support of the labour collective,[7] took the decision to buy up all the remaining assets in 2–3 months. The major stimulus for this decision (and not only for Siberturb, but also for the majority of the others) was the Russian government's decision before 1 October 1992 to

139

base the valuation of main assets on the accounting data for 1 July 1992[8]. The revaluation was based on the balance cost of equipment, buildings and facilities (physical assets), bought or built by the enterprises before 1991; this resulted in a book value increase by 4.5 to 46 times (depending on the types of main asset) and in 1991 the increase was by 3 to 20 times. The assets of the enterprises being privatized in 1992 had to be bought from the state without taking into account this revaluation, and from 1 January 1993 the initial capital belonging to the new shareholding company increased automatically many times. If the workforce postponed privatization of their enterprise until after 1 January 1993 it would be necessary to buy the state or municipal property at a much higher price. As is clear from this discussion, the progress of economic reforms has not served to improve the legitimacy of the government's actions. There is a continuing feeling, persisting from the reforms of the late 1980s, that economic changes are compounding rather than overcoming the problems of Russian industry.

Privatization at enterprise level

The effects of the changes in government policy described above obviously influence behaviour within enterprises. Thus Siberturb bought the assets leased from the state out of its own profits and with vouchers (collected from employees and bought at the stock exchanges) and became a joint stock-company of an open type from 2 February 1993.

It is necessary to note that government organizations themselves appeared unready for large-scale rapid privatization, there was no institutional infrastructure for privatization, or any campaign of mass education. The "rules of the game" were changed constantly: in less than a year (especially from December 1991 to July 1992) more than 10 legislative documents on privatization were issued, and each of them contained significant changes in basic policy. As a result, the management at the company Elmach, for example, began the process of privatization on their own initiative in the autumn of 1991, but finished it only in April 1993. In this period economic staff had to change the plans and revise the project documents. The directorate had to go to the shopfloor three or four times and talk persuasively to the employees time and again in order to secure their approval to continue acting under new conditions.

The situation at Lebags and Matools had already passed through the stage of transformation from state enterprise into leasehold (Lebags in January 1990; Matools in January 1991) and then into the joint-stock company form. It is interesting that Lebags, in which women make up more than 90 per cent of the shop floor and the greater part of the management, chose the collective property option initially (joint-stock company of the closed type), while the mainly male Matools became an open stock company from the very beginning.

In considering the influence of the privatization process on enterprise labour relations, it is necessary to note the following. With such a high privatization tempo, with frequent changes in principles and procedures, the overwhelming majority of enterprises' employees did not understand anything at all about privatization and regarded it as a deception. As a worker commented: "Privatization is robbery and an undertaking which makes people into slaves. Only the top gets something from it. But the top did not operate in the past, as they operate today. As for us, we feel that we are slaves. If we object to the present situation, we'll be fired" (Siberturb). As well as the general economic deterioration, the completely *Bolshevik* approach to implementing privatization as a one-off campaign led to growing mistrust towards any official organizations, and their decisions and actions. Since the enterprise management was, and remains, the representative of power as far as the mass of employees is concerned, this dissatisfaction and mistrust in the majority of the case study enterprises was channelled against top management and against the initiative of its representatives. The antagonism between shop floor workers and the management increased for this reason. Privatization slowed down technical progress at the majority of enterprises. No improvement has been seen in working conditions, which are becoming worse because the enterprises have no money to improve them.

Transformation into joint-stock companies has not changed anything in terms of the relationship of individual employees to property. It is not accidental that the general director of Matools (which was a joint-stock company for almost two years) complained at the conference of shareholders that no ordinary employee had shown himself to be a real co-owner of the enterprise. The situation at Siberturb is similar: the overwhelming majority of the employees do not consider themselves to be the owners of the enterprise. All the majority of employees receive as the result of privatization are the possibility of dividends and of selling their shares at a profit. At present these are unrealistic hopes. Even at the most

141

profitable of the case study enterprises, the 1993 dividends would be less than an average monthly salary. Dividends at the company Matools for 1992 were only 48 per cent of an average monthly salary; at Lebags, 900 roubles for an average employee's share holding (about 7 per cent of the average monthly salary in January 1993). After agitation provoked by voucher and money auctions for the sale of shares of enterprises being privatized, the exchange of shares by investment organizations in Novosibirsk and Krasnoyarsk almost ceased. In the majority of enterprises people have only the possibility of selling their shares to the enterprise through investment-trust companies especially established there. Since top management are usually the founders and the main owners of such companies, this mechanism serves to redistribute shares exclusively to the advantage of top managers. Enterprise directors have gained the most from privatization: they have received real economic freedom in the sense of autonomy from the state ministries, and they are often the main shareholders. In addition, they have a legal basis for strengthening their power base once they have passed through the re-election procedure at the first general meeting of shareholders (which was very difficult for some of them). The shareholders elect the management as their legal representatives, usually for 5 or 3 years. Campaigns to persuade workers to re-invest profits have been started at some enterprises. Of course, it is very difficult to secure their agreement to re-invest profits and capitalize their dividends under present conditions when the majority of employees lack money in their daily life. Hence the strategy of management to exclude employee shareholders from participation in management. As a result, although the workers hold the overwhelming majority of the shares, after privatization workers' representatives are absent from the elected bodies of the new companies.

The economic context and enterprise business strategy

During the period of our research the general economic situation in Russia was worsening. According to official data, the level of industrial output at constant prices, using January 1990 as the base, was 95.47 per cent in 1991; 81.18 per cent in 1992; 65.54 per cent in 1993; and only 63.05 per cent by May 1993.[9] In the summer and autumn of 1993 this depression continued, with approximately the same rates in the raw fuel and manufacturing industries. At enterprise level, however, official statistical data obscures the real situation in industry. These figures are based on the total income of an enterprise including, in particular, profit from barter (especially export–import), trade, and financial operations, which have increased greatly in recent years. The volume of production has decreased much more than the total income in the majority of enterprises. For example, at Siberturb the level of production (in tons of metal) from December 1992 to June 1993 was 32–35 per cent of average monthly output in 1991, and at the end of 1993 it had decreased by at least 1.5 times. Production at Foundry has fallen approximately 10 times in comparison with 1990 levels. At Aero, in the first six months of 1993, the number of passengers and tonnage carried decreased by a half and the number of flights by a third.

In all the manufacturing case study enterprises, 1992 and 1993 were crisis years: debts between enterprises were increasing, production was declining (especially during the second half of 1992), and they traded solely on the basis of advance payments. For these reasons the enterprises were forced to make a number of similar changes. The first was the search for new customers and a gradual change of production profile (for example Matools had been making one kind of machine tool for ships but switched to another type for the agricultural market); and to increase the output of products for which there were solvent customers. This is most clearly shown at Lebags, which produces only consumer goods, and where rapid changes in leather haberdashery products gave the factory stable sales on the internal market, in spite of high prices. The second common point is diversification of production at Elmach, Siberturb, and especially Matools, where not only the output of the traditional production was increased many times, but some new products were also created. The third was to develop new forms of trading operation (at Siberturb, Lebags, and partially at Matools), often on the basis of barter relationships. A further common feature was to seek out opportunities in foreign markets. Here the most notable success was achieved by Elmach and Siberturb. However, the prospects for growth in these markets declined from the summer of 1993. This is shown by the example of Almetal, which exported more than 95 per cent of production and was the most prosperous enterprise studied. From July, the financial position of this enterprise deteriorated very seriously when the cost of energy increased by 3.5 times. In an interview, the director of economics stated: "The world price of aluminium is stabilized, and the total amount of currency that we are receiving every month is also stabilized. But the rouble equivalent will not increase from the summer of 1993 because the State Bank of Russia is artificially suppressing the dollar exchange rate.[10] At the same time, all our prices and costs of production are constantly increasing, on average at 20 per cent a month.[11] The plant has to have 50 billion roubles (at September prices) to work, to continue reconstruction and to maintain the social welfare. But in August and September we had a maximum of 28–29 billion."

The investment situation in most Russian industrial enterprises is in crisis. They have less money to invest in development, re-equipment and new construction than before *perestroika*. From the case study enterprises, the worst situations are at enterprises Elmach and Foundry. These formerly successful enterprises had no money for investment from the middle of 1992, and attempts to find working capital became the main task of their management, with the necessity of offsetting the large and rapid growth of prices and the fall in the purchasing power of salaries and wages. Almetal, an aluminium plant, which increased its investments constantly during the previous two and a half years, was forced to freeze the best part of its work on the reconstruction of the main production area at the end of 1993 and to look for additional money outside the enterprise to finish the construction of three new autonomous enterprises to produce construction materials, such as bricks. Matools, despite a financial situation that is no better than that at Elmach, still invests in development: in 1992 a quarter of the profit was re-invested, and in 1993 the figure was only slightly less. At Lebags, extensive new building construction continues, along with increasing investment. This enterprise carried out a second issue of shares in June 1993 (the only one among the case study companies to do so) with the aim of getting funds for their developing programme.

The next common feature is that in all the enterprises the strategy continues to be formulated by top management. At Lebags it is the exclusive preserve of the general manager. Nevertheless, even at Lebags the top collective executive bodies (such as the Board of Directors or the Executive Board) have started to play a growing role in developing, and especially in implementing enterprise strategy. Representatives of middle management are important here. At Siberturb and Matools, where operating divisions have already achieved a high level of independence, the role of some divisional managers in developing production policy is comparable to that of top management. Our judgement is that this tendency will not only be preserved in the future, but will in fact increase.

It is essential to note that during the period 1991–3 the very rich experience of managing the organization of labour and production, accumulated over many years in Soviet enterprises, began to disintegrate. In conditions where the economic position of the enterprise depends not on the effectiveness of its production but on the chaotic solutions of the government and the vagaries of unstable prices, the traditional strategy of hoarding labour and/or materials becomes senseless or even harmful. These conditions of economic crisis have weakened the traditional mechanisms of the labour process. However, the issue of how control of production will be reconstituted remains an open question.

Thus the prevailing economic context has a number of implications for the emerging structure of interests within the enterprise and related patterns of labour relations. Workers are fearful of losing their jobs and incomes in a situation where the enterprise is no longer able to meet the social needs of the labour collective as it had in the past. This both increases the unity of the collective (because of the threats to job security) and increases tension inside the work group. In many cases this has put the old trade union in the role of trying to consolidate enterprise changes and has reinforced the role of the trade union as a support for management. The argument from the trade union is that now is not the time to struggle. The position of middle management is also changing and new possibilities are opening up for them. In general, there are demands for new skills and competences at all levels.

Restructuring and the position and role of middle management

The difficulties of the economic situation in the mid-1990s, and the strategy of diversification to win new market segments, adopted by the majority of the case study enterprises, press top management towards decentralization and to give their subdivisions greater economic autonomy. The senior managers of Matools and Siberturb understand this very well and defined their goal as transforming their single enterprises into holding companies. This has already happened at Matools, which is now a complex of firms with different degrees of independence, regulated by contracts with joint-stock enterprises and among themselves. At

Siberturb, this process is going more slowly, as divisional managers "ripen" and prepare themselves to manage "independent" businesses. The auxiliary and service divisions not connected directly with the manufacture of core products, normally get independence first. At Siberturb the situation is difficult because senior management wants to preserve the enterprise as a unit. However, the pressure of economic conditions and the growing demand of the departmental chiefs have forced top management to give some of the departments the status of plants. Most division managers at Siberturb and Elmach are seeking quite openly to increase their independence. At Matools the situation is more complicated: the managers of firms that have not so far received legal independence do not seek it, and the managers of independent firms do not show any enthusiasm for it. This can be explained by the fact that the controlling shares are held by the joint-stock company, Matools, and this severely restricts the firm's independence. The general manager still uses administrative management methods. For example, he can fire a manager of an "independent" firm whenever he wishes without consulting anyone else. Independence is stimulated somewhat by 40–60 per cent of profit received from outside orders being maintainted by the firm, but this incentive is reduced substantially by the contribution to overheads exacted by the holding company. The situation at Lebags is very different. Financial relationships with its subdivisions are undeveloped, and management is against any degree of divisional independence. While there are no departmental managers who seek independence, those managers who expressed their interest in this idea to the management have already been "made to leave".

The present rate of inflation and market instability constrain the development of internal financial relations at the enterprises. In these conditions, the systems of internal cost-accounting that were operating have begun to be curtailed at Almetal, Elmach and Foundry. In a situation where the planned budget of the enterprise has to be recalculated several times a month, it has become almost impossible in practice to transfer it to the subdivisions. It is possible to cope with the problem in centralized conditions, but there is no way to do it at the subdivision level. The position with the wage fund is the same.

It has to be emphasized that senior management of the enterprises have strengthened their position as a result of broader economic processes in Russia. Some Western researchers consider that there are only few changes in the position of middle management (Clarke & Fairbrother

1993c), but the data from our research shows that these managers are the most likely group to challenge senior management, mainly because of changes in the system of labour relations at the enterprise. Although the position of the middle management differs between the case study enterprises, the main trends are clear, as is shown below.

Middle managers strive increasingly to gain economic independence and to transform their divisions into independent enterprises. There are several reasons for this. A sharp decline has occurred in the financial-economic situation of many processing and engineering enterprises since the second half of 1991. Many of the senior managers were forced to set departmental managers the goal of providing finances both for their divisions and for the enterprise as a whole, and gave them a certain degree of independence to do this (for example, in Siberturb, Elmach and Matools). Many of the divisional managers succeeded in coping with the situation and prevented their workshops from standing idle, but having secured outside orders and reorganized the work of their subdivisions, they resisted the idea of giving a considerable part of the income earned to the enterprise budget, and of having the salaries of their employees determined by senior management. In 1989–91 many of the managers, and some of the subdivision specialists, set up (or took part in setting up) co-operatives made up of different types of small enterprises, both inside their subdivisions and outside. Noting how specialists from the sales department operate, they realized that in the present market conditions they can sell their products directly without a special enterprise-wide service, and often more profitably than can the sales department (for example, Elmach, Matools, Almetal and Foundry).

There is no interest for a real specialist to work only as a line manager, especially in comparison with his or her Western colleagues with whom s/he now has opportunities to deal, both in Russia and abroad. Clearly managers of large departments have been aware for a long time of the shortcomings of their work simply as line managers with limited authority; in present conditions, they have only administrative methods at their disposal. The management superstructure becomes redundant, and maintaining labour and technological discipline is then their main task. These latter factors become meaningless in the present situation where the enterprises operate at a completely erratic pace and increase their conflicts with subordinates (for example, in Elmach, Matools, Almetal and Foundry).

Middle managers are usually younger and more ambitious than the senior ones. The overwhelming majority have higher technical education in their field of work (usually a technological background) and because of their middle management position, they are fairly well informed about many aspects of the enterprise's operation. They want a greater role in developing the business strategies of the enterprise. They have learnt to use their position in the management hierarchy of the enterprise: in relation to top management they put the opinions of their workers to the Executive Board, but in relation to the workforce they present themselves as the unwilling conduits of senior management's orders. They try constantly to show their employees that they are practically the same hired people as the workers, and for this reason they appear to be more trustworthy in the eyes of the employees than top management. In their understanding of privatization and share holding, they are far ahead of their employees and often deal personally with these questions in their divisions. Many middle managers have specific plans to use the emerging mechanisms and elected management structures of the joint-stock company to gain higher personal status in the management hierarchy and more favourable working conditions and wages for their divisions (for example, in Elmach, Almetal and Foundry). Our observations show that in the early 1990s middle managers have started to perceive themselves as a unified occupational group. They have also begun to take certain organizational steps in this direction; for example, by the creation of departmental managers' councils, clubs for managers, and business clubs where the main roles are often played by departmental managers. The role of middle managers is critical to the transformation of Russian enterprises, as they will be responsible operationally for directing the change in systems of labour control. However, as our research indicates, and other commentators confirm (Clarke et al. 1993; Filtzer 1991), at present there seems to be little incentive for middle managers to completely abandon their traditional dependence upon the workforce. In fact, in conditions of such uncertainty, the workforce may provide middle management with its best bulwark against senior managements' power.

Employment and wages policy

The majority of enterprises studied had to reduce the number of employees because of considerable cutbacks in production. However, this has generally been done in an indirect way: the majority of the employees at Elmach were given unpaid leave when they were working a shortened week; at Lebags there was job rotation as well as changes in personnel; at Siberturb wage funds were placed at the disposal of divisions and it was for them to decide how many employees they need. At the same time, the conditions for hiring new workers were made much stricter. As a result, at all the enterprises there is a growing feeling of anxiety connected with mass workforce redundancies. Nevertheless, the majority of managers consider mass redundancies in the years to come as being unrealistic: "Mass redundancies could have been demanded by external owners who are interested only in increasing the profit. We don't have owners of this kind at present and there will be none in the near future. As for the management, it would not start this painful and unpleasant procedure of its own accord. They would sooner introduce a shortened week (as it used to be). The transition to a joint-stock company does not change anything, especially when the labour collective has the controlling shares" (deputy economic director).

Clarke & Fairbrother (1993b) explain this situation at the enterprises they studied as a clear demonstration of the paternalistic attitudes of Russian management. In our opinion it is opportunistic; in many enterprises management adopt this policy not because they identify with their labour collectives and consider themselves to be responsible for the future of every employee, but simply because it is a cheaper way (in both the moral and the material sense) of reducing labour. The example of Siberturb is typical: 60 per cent of workers who should have been dismissed as redundant in April 1993 were put into an operational reserve and most of them did not return to the enterprise. The most favourable situation is now observed at Matools. Here labour turnover has always been high (more than 30 per cent a year) but the total number of employees was decreased only slightly at the time of introducing the joint-stock structures (8 per cent during 1989–91). Later the number of employees began to increase: by 157 people or (20 per cent) in 1992, and there was also a small increase in 1993.

There are some differences in the wages and salaries situation at the enterprises. These differences would be much greater if the second sample of enterprises were included. Unfortunately, the research in these enterprises was carried out at different times, so a strict comparison is not possible in the labour payment situation. However, a qualitative comparison *is* possible. In 1992 and 1993 wage increases to all groups and categories of employees took place in all the enterprises (almost every month). It was not necessary for workers or trade unions to take any special action to secure this. Wages were increased on the initiative of management, with the sole aim of compensating for the constant growth of consumer prices and thus retaining (in anticipation of a better future) the greater part of their skilled workforce. However, no enterprise was able to succeed in this aim. Comparing today's wages with those of 1988-9 (people usually make the comparison with these years, which was the last time the economic situation was relatively stable), we can see that the prices of consumer goods for everyday use doubled in 1990 on average, increased in 1991 by 3.5 times, in 1992 by 30 times, and by the end of 1993 a further 9 times. So, to maintain the purchasing power of wages they would have to increase sevenfold in 1991, a hundred and eighty-fold in 1992, and one thousand eight hundred-fold to the end of 1993. Skilled workers at the case study enterprises normally received 350-450 roubles per month in 1988-9; in order to keep that level they needed to receive 3,000 roubles at the beginning of 1992; 35,000 to the middle of 1992; 85,000-90,000 at the beginning of 1993; and 295,000-315,000 in the middle of 1993. Such figures were achieved only at Almetal. Elmach lagged behind these figures and much lower wages were paid at Siberturb, Lebags and Matools (see Table 6.2).

Comparing the wages with the monthly minimum consumer budget for a working man[12], it is clear that only the workers at Almetal and Elmach were able to maintain consumption at the given level, not only for themselves but also for the members of their families. At the rest of the enterprises, the employees were only able to provide for themselves. In general, workers talk about take home pay. These figures take no account of consumer goods or foodstuffs provided in the enterprise at subsidized prices, nor of annual bonuses. It should be noted that total social income, that is, the total amount of benefits, is not now calculated at any

Table 6.2 Estimates of the wage level for high-skilled workers of the main occupations at the case study enterprises ('000s of roubles per month).

Enterprise	Begining of 1992	Middle of 1992	Beginning of 1993	Middle of 1993
ALMETAL	10.1	18.5	90.0	390.0
ELMACH	6.4	19.1	51.0	170.0
MATOOLS	1.7	6.7	21.7	–
SIBERTURB	1.5	6.5	13.0	34.0
LEBAGS	0.8	3.6	21.0	52.0

of the case study enterprises; only the maintenance costs of the social welfare are taken into account to some extent. According to the calculations received, this sum accounts for 30–40 per cent of annual salary. If we also take into account barter trade operations with foodstuffs and other goods conducted by the social service section and the enterprise's trade union, then the total sums will amount to not less than a half the official salary (to compare: in the 1970s, social benefits in industry were about 15–20 per cent of the worker's total income from an enterprise).

It is necessary to note that constant salary and wage increases in 1991–3 were provided by enterprise management, even though it destroyed any link between productivity and wages. More significantly, the link between wages and skills was broken so that the meaning of the terms "skill" and "qualification" became unclear. If it takes 10 years of education to be a professional technologist or designer; 5–7 years to become a highly skilled mechanic, but only 3–4 months to become a broker, and if the broker's income is 10 times higher than that of the designer or mechanic, then the prestige of real qualifications falls to almost zero.

Management's aim to keep confidential what people receive as wages is seen clearly at the majority of enterprises. A typical explanation is: "Let them stop looking in each other's pockets, let them look into their own and think how to earn more!" Most employees understand this action by management as an attempt to strengthen their own power, to increase their own incomes and to weaken the unity both of the workers and the other groups of employees. It is interesting that this attempt stimulates the development of the contract system of recruitment and payment (first for senior and middle managers, then for specialists, and next for other groups of workers), at the case study enterprises. However, neither employees nor management understand the essence of a contract, namely that there is mutual agreement between employee and employer. So, at Elmach for example, at the beginning of 1993, there was a campaign to draw up contracts with all shop managers. It was done in the following way: specialists from the labour department produced the text of the standard contract which was sent to all shop managers with the opportunity to make comments and to sign. Only two or three of them made any comment – the other 25 simply signed the standard text. Subsequently, the general director signed all the contracts. There was no bargaining with those who made comments; these were simply left in files at the labour department.

151

In the majority of case study enterprises, manual labour is still rated higher than qualified work; workers of the basic professions and basic departments receive higher salaries than the workers in auxiliary shops and the services division. As before, the stereotype is perpetuated that the one who participates directly in the manufacturing process is more important to an enterprise than, not only the maintenance workers, but also engineers, economists and managers in general. Contemporary management understands the need to take some steps in the direction of changing these stereotypes. Thus at Lebags, at the beginning of 1992 bonuses for qualified labour were introduced and the seamstresses grades were raised considerably, and at the time of writing some of the skilled workers receive wages comparable with shop managers. A uniform 18-grade wage scale was introduced at Elmach in the autumn of 1993 and as a result the wages of workers in the basic and auxiliary shops became almost equal. At Siberturb, a similar result was achieved by decentralizing all wage issues to departmental level. It should be noted that these ideas have started to penetrate the workers' collectives. Thus, the majority already agree that line managers should receive a slightly higher salary than they themselves do. Nevertheless, when the difference becomes twofold, it is immediately perceived as being unjust. From this comes a natural desire for workers to cut down managerial expenses and reduce the number of specialists, who are considered to be a burden on their work.

Trade unions

The trade unions, which could have played a major role in the articulation of employees' interests, now find themselves in deep crisis. They have been eliminated at Lebags and Matools, and at the other enterprises have completely lost the trust of their members. In the latter cases they have turned into something between a "consumer co-operative society" and a department subordinated to the deputy director on social issues. This situation at enterprise level is explained by the fact that the single trade union structure which existed in the former Soviet Union has disintegrated, and the top trade union bodies have almost completely lost their links with the branch organizations. Within the limits of this chapter it is not possible to discuss the general situation of the trade union movement in Russia (see Gordon et al. 1993). In our view, the position of the top trade union structures is more clearly visible at the regional, rather than the national, level. The Novosibirsk Regional Trade Union Federation (NRTUF) was created in February 1991. The organising principle was that it was built "bottom-up" from organizations upon which the higher levels were dependent. In the large unions, regional committees were created, and in the small unions, regional councils. NRTUF is an inter-branch co-ordinating body which produces only recommendations or proposals; it has no power as such. The basic organizations keep 80–90 per cent of the income received from different sources, 10–20 per cent is given to their regional committee, and the latter gives part of this to NRTUF (in the mid-1990s about 2 per cent of the organizations' basic income). One result is that the regional trade union newspaper is always on the verge of closure. At the beginning of 1993, the membership of NRTUF was approximately 930,000 blue- and white-collar workers, and some 70,000 students: this is 250 thousand less than in 1992, but the total number of employees in the NRTUF branches of the region decreased by the same amount. Only 55,000 people left the trade union in 1992.

The NRTUF'S relations with the centre are based on the same principle as between the basic organization and the regional federation. The NRTUF is a member of the Federation of Independent Trade Unions of Russia (FITUR), and the chairman of NRTUF is included in the FITUR Council. There are also 14 trade union associations in Novosibirsk that do not belong to NRTUF. The largest are the trade union of railroad workers (approximately 150,000 members) and the former *Minsred-mash* (about 35,000 members) which used to belong directly to the All-Union Central Council of Trade Unions (AUCCTU). All the others (including the Association of Socialist Trade Unions (Sotsprof), which was created in 1990) are very small and do not have any influence on labour relations in the region or city of Novosibirsk. The air traffic controllers and pilots are confined to air transport.[13]

The priority of the primary organizations proclaimed in 1990 by AUCCTU, has led today to the almost complete separation of regional and central trade union organization from the enterprises. As a result, the top bodies lost the usual managerial levers and attended to purely adminis-trative work. This is not confined to the Novosibirsk region. The chair-man of the trade union committee of one of the largest Krasnoyarsk enterprises said in an interview: "The Regional Committee is separated from the enterprises – they do not come to us and do not involve us in any of their activities. They only do administrative work and we stopped thinking about them. It seems to be good – they do not interfere with our work, but we got accustomed to relations and want to receive from them help, prompting, organizational influence. As the result our mine-metallurgy trade union separated from FITUR, and our relations with the Regional Trade Union Committee became very shaky." Consequently, any significant and mass organizational work at the enterprise and regional levels ceased, so the effectiveness of NRTUF activity is very weak: "If we try to organize any significant common action, at most 3 per cent of people will participate, and 97 per cent will stay outside." It would seem that in this situation there should be an open discussion about the role, function and structure of the trade unions in the period of transition to the market economy, but there is no such discussion. The leader of NRTUF explained this as follows: first, the main trade union functions are known to the activists, but the reason is that trade union leaders themselves are not interested in such a discussion: "If this issue is discussed, the question will arise: who are the leaders of enterprise trade unions, why aren't these people seen and heard, why do they work mainly for the Director on social questions? And if the Chairman of the Regional Committee would offer such a discussion with shop floor workers, they would put so many questions that he could not answer. But the people in the trade union leadership are mainly the same. And why not – it is good to sit in the regional committee or in the federation. We have set our own salaries. The work is not too hard and there is practically no responsibility, but there is a car, an office, and invitations! What is the necessity to get involved?"

Relations between the NRTUF and enterprise management are complicated. On the one hand, when there is the need to press the government on issues, the management comes to the regional trade union and proposes organizing action. Nevertheless, when such action is successful (as, for example, in the spring and summer of 1992), and the situation in the enterprises is eased, the directors then begin to restrict their relations with trade unions: "No director needs a strong trade union which could be a counterbalance to him. And if one of the union leaders challenges the management, he will quickly be isolated from the collective and his position taken away. And where will he get afterwards? We are not strong enough to guarantee his defence: the trade union committee at the instrumental plant was defended, but at *Vega* the conflict between the general director and the union chairman ended with the director's victory and we couldn't help him" (Trade Union official). It is obvious that in this situation ordinary union members know little about the work of the top union bodies. Little information comes from the regional committees and most of the material sent to them by the regional structure stays in their offices because they and the chairman of the primary organization seldom meet. If a paper goes to the primary trade union committee nobody from the shop floor will ever see it. The effectiveness of collective action decreased in 1993. In the summer months the FITUR and its regional divisions prepared (for the autumn) a series of mass protests against the policy of thè president and government. A special statement of the FITUR Co-ordinating Committee on Collective Action (June 24) was issued, where it was noted that "the government of pragmatists" does not justify hope, and that it chose a very narrow way to fight inflation by wage limitation and restriction of the social programmes. The main union demands were also included in this statement:

(a) enterprise productivity should be encourage by the system of taxation, and loans;

(b) compensation for unpaid wages should take the inflation rate in the period of delay into account;

(c) there should be laws on the minimum income, the payment system and the struggle against corruption; and

(d) state prices on energy, some food products, medicines, housing and public transport should be controlled.

The Novosibirsk Federation also published the statement (approved on 9 July), repeating these four demands with the addition of tax relief on profit used for investment; credit for defence enterprises; a freeze on prices for energy, raw and basic materials; assistance for working capital of production enterprises; protection measures for agricultural enterprises; long-term credit for the reconstruction and development of the processing industry, for improvement and for prepayment for agricultural products that are delivered to the state resources; and for encouraging investment. In conclusion, the statement declared that if these demands were not met, NRTUF Co-ordinating Committee on Collective Action would begin to promote mass protest actions, including strikes. This programme of collective action planned by the trade union was not carried out because of the famous tragic events of 3–5 October 1993 in Moscow. But it is necessary to note that the NRTUF leaders were not sure themselves that the actions planned would be successful: "It seems that there are many ways to influence public opinion and different powerful bodies. To gather, for example, 100 lorries and drive across the city with lights and slogans – half the city population would see them; or to organize a half-hour traffic block on the main street; or to move agricultural machines on the Novosibirsk–Barnaul motorway and stop traffic for half an hour. And to proclaim – if nothing is done to improve the situation, tomorrow we shall close the motorway for two hours, and then for a whole day. But these measures will produce results only if people really support our actions and if we proclaim that today we shall stop 10 enterprises, tomorrow 40 and then 100, and carry it out, the authorities would take account of us and the government would bargain with us and fulfil their promises. But if we could not do this, it would be the end and nobody would ever respect us again. But we have no such firmness today. How [can we] call out on strike the workers from transport, power stations, meat or chocolate factories if their wages are now 3–4 times more than in the machine building industry? For so many years we have heard about workers' solidarity, but now it is practically gone!" The situation described here is not typical for all regions of Russia. Based on mass media reports and the views of specialists who study the workers' movement, it is clear that in coal and oil regions the trade unions are much more integrated and influential. But in those regions where manufacturing industries are concentrated, the situation is very similar to that in Novosibirsk or Krasnoyarsk.

The basic union organizations lack any central leadership, and try to develop their activities and establish their place in the constantly changing system of labour relations in the enterprises. Typically, the characteristic roles at an enterprise are as follows. Although the union is liquidated at some enterprises, there is no reason to expect that they will disappear completely. In the seven case studies, the trade union was suspended only at two. At Lebags the awakening green shoots of consciousness (both at "bottom" and "top" levels) that it was necessary to establish a new trade union organization began to grow about a year after the earlier union was dissolved. Workers believe that it should represent their interests and be independent of management. Managers think that the union should be a channel for discussing and resolving problems of vital importance to both management and employees. The majority of union members do not leave their organizations – numbers leaving were not more than 1–2 per cent and often less than 1 per cent. In interviews, we often heard the opinion that many workers would leave the union if the deduction of subscriptions from wages was changed: "If people paid union subscriptions themselves, they would see how much they pay for nothing, and resign." This does not seem to be a convincing argument. The union subscription for a worker, even of the most prosperous enterprises, is equivalent to 1 or 2 bottles of vodka, and if anybody leaves the union they lose much more than this. There are significant changes in union functions at the enterprises. They no longer deal with the mobilization of workers to carry out production plans, and they have ceased to distribute accommodation because no flats are built now and they have lost the social insurance function (i.e. sick leave payment). In 1991–2 the unions increased their commercial activities (for example, barter deals and buying goods and food for resale to their members), but in 1993 this slowed down, (If there are market conditions, let's pay the full wage to the employees and let them spend this money as they wish and pay the real prices!"). Other unions gave this work to the management.

According to the changes made to the Labour Code, it has not been necessary since 1992 for the union to give consent to dismissals for disciplinary offences, and trade unions now detach themselves from individual dismissals. Union meetings are diminishing – the labour collectives meet twice a year at most for collective agreement conferences. The direct consequence is that the workers' awareness of matters of enterprise and union organization has decreased significantly. Enterprise newspapers do not improve this situation because workers do not read them. Nobody at the enterprises, including the union leaders themselves, sees the union as an organization that defines, expresses and protects the employees' interests in opposition to employers. On the contrary, the idea prevails that the unions' highest value is the interest not of its members, but that of the enterprise itself, or of a certain "commonwealth". It is very significant that the opinions of both managers and union leaders on the question of what the trade union should be are almost identical, while at the same time they are contrary to the opinions of the workers. Such unity between union and management is a product of the Soviet "state-managed" society that existed for so many years. While enterprises were state property, it was necessary to defend the interests of the labour collective against the state – from the centrally determined tariffs and wage rates that did not permit normal labour payment, from prices imposed from above, and from profits appropriated by the ministry which prevented the enterprise from improving labour conditions. It was necessary for the union to rally management and the Party organization to secure any success in this fight with the state. Today, the basis for this alliance has gone and this inhibits the development of a model of labour relations appropriate for the new conditions.

Generally, the unions were fairly heavily involved in the campaign for transformation into joint-stock companies, now the only public structure that embraces the whole workforce of the enterprise. Both the campaign and the subscriptions for employee shares were organized by the union. One union leader was usually elected to the Shareholders' Council or the Board of Directors (the latter is appointed in the joint-stock company standard charter to elect the management body for the owners). But at Almetal, the trade union leaders went further. The labour collective chose the second option of transformation into a joint-stock company, the workforce (management included) bought 51 per cent of the shares of the initial capital for 1.7% of the nominal price and created a special partnership of Almetal employees to manage these shares as a single block, and the chairman of the union committee became the head of this partnership. "We formed this partnership with the sole aim of protecting the interests of employee–shareholders in the main issue – that their enterprise should work well, be profitable, and that they would receive high wages and not fear losing jobs. And if this is the main interest, the union has to lead in the partnership and to participate in the council of shareholders trying to implement the idea of real democracy, at least in a small way."

Union members themselves have little idea of the nature of the trade unionism they need. There is no acceptance of the former conception of a trade union as a "school of communism", but nobody tries to establish organizations of other types which would meet the requirements of its members. Trade unions will only be able to change when this is fully understood by the members. As pointed out by the head of one of the shop Union committees: "The trade union we now have at the enterprise is the one the employees deserve!"

Tripartism and labour relations at national level

The decree of the Russian Federation's President "On social partnership and resolving labour disputes" formed the basis for the development of collaboration, not only between trade unions and the management of enterprises, but also at a more general level. It is now necessary to conclude national general agreements on social-economic problems, and also branch and regional agreements, every year. The federal, and some branch, Tripartite Commissions were established at the end of 1991 and the beginning of 1992 to develop and control these agreements. In June 1992, of the 14 places in the federal Commission occupied by the trade unions, FITUR had nine places; Sotsprof three; and independent trade unions of mine workers and air traffic controllers, one each. The activity of this commission is, however, insignificant: much time has been spent on organizational issues, and the implementation of decisions of the Commission is very limited. For example, the commission devoted seven meetings over two months to developing the General Tripartite Agreement for 1992, but at the beginning of 1993 it emerged that of 50 provisions, only 15 were fulfilled completely and 14 partially, while the most important remained only on paper (*Trud* 1993).

All three parties to the discussions are responsible for this poor performance. The trade unions very often took conflicting positions; on many issues, the FITUR position was directly opposed to that of the new trade union associations. On the most significant social problems on the agenda there was no quorum on the government side. The employers began to emerge as an independent force from the end of the 1980s, when the Law on Co-operatives was adopted (1987) which gave a strong thrust to the new co-operative movement. The first associations of co-operators and leasors also emerged at the end of the 1980s. In 1990–1 different organizations of private entrepreneurs began to appear, and many of them joined the Business Congress. At the beginning of 1992, the former Scientific–Industrial Union (formed in 1989) was transformed into The Russian Union of Industrialists and Entrepreneurs (RUIE). In November 1992 there was a decision to create an Association of Privatized and Private Enterprises. But in the federal Tripartite Commission the entrepreneurial organizations were only partially represented, and they participated unevenly in its work. Representatives of the enterprise directors are generally in coalition with the FITUR and demand different privileges for existing industry. On the other hand, the representatives of financial, trade and mediation groups often adopt opposing positions, and use their participation in the Commission for personal publicity and prestige. Since the summer of 1993 there has been some improvement in the work of the Commission: issues are more fully elaborated, and outside specialists and consultants participate in its meetings. The seminar "social partnership, collective bargaining and privatization" organized in April 1993 by the ILO had a definite influence on the

Commission. The National General Tripartite Agreement of 1993 shows more harmony. Its main goals are:
  (a) to prevent the fall in production, to strengthen the state influence on socio-economic stabilization, to establish market relations and to develop labour and entrepreneurial activity;
  (b) to implement an active employment policy;
  (c) to reduce the gap between the cost of living and the incomes of the population, and to develop the motivation of productive labour; and
  (d) to provide labour and health protection at work and the ecological security of the population.
  In the General Agreement there are seven basic sections:
  (a) economic stabilization;
  (b) employment policy and labour market;
  (c) incomes and living standards;
  (d) social protection of the population;
  (e) labour protection and ecological security;
  (f) development of the social partnership system; and
  (g) general provisions (term of the agreement's control and fulfilment and the parties' responsibilities).
  However, the provisions of the agreement are very general or largely unrealizable.
  Branch agreements are more characteristic of Russian practice because of the branch structure of production and trade union organization that existed for many years. In production industries in 1992, both sides intended to provide in these agreements guarantees for the production processes' materials supplies, favourable credits, and to establish minimum wage levels above those guaranteed by the state (Gordon et al. 1993). However, in 1993 the situation changed, and with it these agreements. This is illustrated by the example of the agreement between the Central Council of the Trade Union of the Mine–metallurgy Industry, the Committee for Metallurgy, and the Ministry of Labour, which was signed on 15 February 1993. This document looks more like a real agreement between relatively independent partners than the former branch collective agreements, which were largely formal. First of all, the mutual obligations and responsibilities of the parties are specified: that is, the minimum guarantees approved by the Agreement to be incorporated into enterprise collective agreements; the Committee on Metallurgy is to send to the trade union Central Council full information on decisions of the Board of the Committee, on the socio-economic situa-

tion and the development of the branch; employers are to avoid unnecessary job reductions and to consult the trade union on all issues of reduction; and the trade union will not organize strikes on issues covered by the Agreement if a positive solution can be found. Beyond these obligations the Agreement includes eight other sections: labour relations (the role of the collective agreement is defined and the Trade Union recognized as the representative of the employees); hours of work; labour payments; pensions, rewards, privileges and compensations; holidays; employment; labour safety; guarantees for trade union bodies and activities. All the provisions of this Agreement are specific and establish uniform norms of labour relations for the industry. In conclusion, one can say that the national general agreement is little more than a wish list, the overall significance of the provisions is small. The branch level, formerly the key one of organization, is still significant in industries where large enterprises predominate.

Tripartism and collective bargaining in Siberia

In Novosibirsk and Krasnoyarsk there are regional agreements. In Novosibirsk there were two parties to the agreement: the trade union and the regional government, because an employers' organization did not exist in the region. The first regional agreement was signed in 1991, but in 1992 the government refused to sign an agreement because of the unstable and uncertain economic situation and the high rate of inflation. However, in July 1993, they decided to sign. The NRTUF took the initiative in developing this agreement, and their specialist wrote the draft which the government representative signed without any additions to the agreement.

Alternatively, in Krasnoyarsk all three parties participated in negotiating the regional agreement in March 1993. This agreement had four sections. The first, Economic Stabilization and Social–Labour Relations, contains mutual obligations on the participants to support enterprises that produce consumer goods, and their production for regional needs; to improve the food supply of the population and to help agricultural enterprises in their spring and autumn operations; to collaborate with the reform strategy of the region; and to decrease social tensions in the labour collective. The second section is devoted to the problem of minimizing unemployment: specifically to allocate special funds from the regional budget for the creation of new jobs, and the organization of public works and unemployment benefit. It also provides a procedure for relating the rate of redundancies to the level of unemployment in the region: it is recommended that redundancies should be postponed for one month if unemployment is 3–5 per cent, and for six months if it is 11 per cent or more. The third section, Supporting the Standard of Life and Guarantee of the Social Defence for Employees and Population, is very detailed. It provides for improving the system of regional regulation of wages (incomes); developing a system of basic consumer budgets for different groups of population and different subregions of the Krasnoyarsk region; allocating special funds for improving the health of working people and their children, for social security and for providing treatment and rest for the weakest groups of the population; establishing a tax on organizations for education; providing expertise on labour conditions and ecology for building, developing or reconstructing enterprises; and collective agreements and higher social guarantees for compensation in the case of accident or occupational disease. It is also pointed out that the parties demand an increase in the tax threshold, and a decrease in the general level of profit tax in order to free from taxation those parts of profit that will be spent on labour protection and ecological improvements. The final section concerns the implementation of the Agreement, the responsibilities of the parties for this, their duty to inform each other and the regional population about it, and to encourage all other trade union and employers' associations to support the Agreement. It is stressed that all conflicts and strikes related to the problems included in this Agreement are forbidden while the terms of the Agreement remain in force.

Collective bargaining at enterprise level

According to the present research no effective or stable bargaining systems have yet appeared at enterprise level. The basic reason for the absence of negotiations is that the management's power in the enterprises has definitely strengthened, and there is no influential opposing force (in the form of a trade union or other organization which would articulate employees' interests). Nevertheless, some changes in the system of official relations between trade union and management are taking place at many enterprises. The contents of the traditional enterprise collective agreement is changing and the number of sections and appendices are being reduced drastically. These now regulate only the issues of wages, labour and health control, and expenditure on social development and consumption funds. Gradually, the details of production tasks are disappearing from the collective agreement: "We don't now write down the questions of where to install this particular machine tool." On the other hand, questions of wages are worked out in much greater detail than before. It is, however, necessary to stress that at Lebags and Matools, where there are no trade unions, the wages depend much more on management decisions. Increasingly, collective agreements resemble real agreements and not a mixture of declarations and plans for the undertaking. The mutual obligations of the parties are detailed in them. The procedures for the elaboration of collective agreements are also beginning to change. From our interview with the Chairman of Almetal's trade union committee: "Before, every year we drafted the content of the collective agreement on the previous year's pattern. The wages department and other services prepared figures, and the draft was put to the conference, where it was confirmed. Later, nobody looked at this document and its fulfilment was only checked before the next conference. Now everything is quite different. We went to every big workshop and convened the trade union activists (in workshop No. 3, for example, there were 200 people) and analyzed very carefully all the questions and remarks that came from the collectives. The collectives decided what could be solved in the shop, what should be sent to the plant level, and what was simply far-fetched. Then in a special commission we discussed all the details of those questions that were left for the top level. As a result, only 30 per cent of the issues that we supported have not been resolved, and this was because our enterprise had not got sufficient money. Now both employees and management study the collective agreement and keep it to hand for reference." At the same time, employees' interest in collective agreements is declining. The discussion at the workshop meetings and all-plant conferences have become even more formalized and are resolved by mutual agreement. Thus, at Siberturb, no sooner had the economic director told the conference, "Do not worry, you won't have a salary lower than now" than there was a unanimous vote for the "raw" text of the agreement. On the whole, the collective agreement still remains a formal document which cannot be used to resolve any disputed questions in court.

Labour relations and the articulation of interests

The unfavourable economic conditions intensify the divergent interests of different groups of employees. We think it is important to stress that the trade unions do not recognize this differentiation and consider all employees to be a unified community without contradictions. Formerly, the myth of "socialist property" concealed the real control exercised by the state bureaucracy. Traditionally, the lines of division and conflict in the field of labour relations at the enterprises were: workers against managers (at all levels), specialists and office workers; the employees of production divisions (including the specialists and division managers) against the enterprise office; all the employees in basic production against the auxiliary shops and service employees; long-service employees against young and new employees. The conflictual nature of these relations was concealed by the general conception of the "labour collective", the higher administrative body which approved (legally or illegally) the profit earned by an enterprise and, in this way – to use Marxist terminology – played the role of exploiter in relation to the enterprise. This state exploitation became very weak (but did not disappear) after the disintegration of the command–administrative system, and enterprises were transformed into independent joint-stock companies. This changed at once the content of all the former intra-enterprise divisions; the division between the top enterprise management and all the other employees became the main division. The main divisions now are between senior management and middle management, and between workers and management.

Top management has achieved practically unlimited power at the enterprise; they pay little attention to the growing tensions in relations with the base, as they do not see any alternative power centre in the enterprise. In the past they occupied in the system of enterprise labour relations the position of the owners of capital, who exploited the labour force; now they remain the initiators and moving power of all the changes in their enterprises. The fact that the capital is now joint-stock does not change anything. On the contrary, the paradox is that although they hold less than a controlling block of shares, the senior managers in reality hold all the power in the joint-stock company. For the most part, ordinary employees consider the shares of "their" enterprise to be a kind of savings bank book, or even as a "loyalty certificate", and have only a vague idea about their rights as shareholders (and about their rights in general). Nevertheless, it is significant that top management do not perceive themselves to be exploiters: thus, strategies that would be acceptable to any Western capitalist are rejected by Russian top managers. This may change in time, but at present they do not even feel it is necessary to present annual reports to their "shareholders".

As for middle managers, they all face a hard choice today. First, to force their way into the "top division" of the joint-stock capital's managers; the small amount of shares they possess is, of course, insufficient for this, but the place they occupy in the management structure, their commercial experience, their formal and informal links inside and outside the enterprise, their solidarity with the other managers, and influence on the workers, give them good opportunities to force their way in if they should choose. An alternative second approach is to leave the "playing field" and to become a pure manager, the channel of the top level's commands to the shop floor, losing for ever the former cosy position of the social alibi of the workers. The majority of managers choose the first and this dooms them to tactical opposition to the "top division" into which they want to force their way.

The position of workers has changed radically: their standard of living is lower, they have lost wages and additional income possibilities in comparison with senior management and some services; and to a large degree, their interest in their work has been lost. They are afraid (at some of the enterprises they are under pressure) of reduced production; the management treats them more strictly ("And if you don't like it, you can leave!"). The main change is that they have lost their hegemonic status and are discovering at last their real status as hired workers. The recognition of this fact is very painful for them.

Changes in the positions of other social and professional groups are played out in the power field of the enterprise. The status of enterprise office employees has changed considerably and in different directions. The greatest losers are engineers: their high, but very narrow, specialized qualification is not now in demand, and not valued; very often it is difficult for them to find a job and additional earnings anywhere else. On the other hand, the status of economic and commercial services has become noticeably higher. Older employees, who used to be secure, are now considered to be some of the most insecure. It is much more difficult for them to adapt to new conditions, requirements and norms of life and work; and the idea of private property as well as the principles of economic independence are alien to them. They are the first to be laid off and they cannot hope for a new place; they are the ones who were unprotected by management when the Party committees were dissolved and the traditional trade unions found themselves in deep crisis. That is why the majority of these older workers are psychologically distressed, afraid for their future, frightened of privatization and, in general, any changes in the enterprise. Unskilled young people have always been in a bad position in the enterprise, but now their position is becoming even worse. As before, they are mainly involved in unskilled and less well paid work, and as their needs are greater and they are worse provided for than people of average age, they feel more strongly than do others about the lack of wages. As for employment elsewhere, they often do not have the necessary qualifications. The possibilities of studying and improving their qualifications have become noticeably worse; they have lost their organization (the Young Communist League), which did something to protect their interests in the past. On the other hand the young workers and specialists whose skills are defined not so much by experience as by education (for example, programmers, or adjusters of complicated equipment), have raised their status at the enterprise. This is reflected in their relatively greater readiness for change and the fact that some of them leave for commerce.

Overall, it should be stressed that the dependence of ordinary employees on the management has increased sharply. In the past they could express and protect their interests through the enterprise organizations, the trade unions, the Communist Party, the Young Communist League, and Councils of the Labour Collectives (CLCs). The Party and Young Communist league organizations have been liquidated. In the seven enterprises studied at the beginning of our research there were CLCs in only four, Aero, Siberturb, Foundry and Matools. But when enterprises were transformed into joint-stock companies, the CLCs at Siberturb and Foundry were dissolved and at Matools it was reconstructed into the Production (Enterprise) Council. This council signed the collective agreement on behalf of the staff. Its main task is to "maintain civil peace at the enterprise", but its authority at the enterprise is very low. It is threatened by workers, specialists and lower and middle managers in the same way as the trade union had been, which was subsequently dissolved. The most active workers and middle-managers of Aero and Siberturb expressed some hope for the articulation and protection of their interests through participation in electing management bodies of joint-stock companies, including "The Employees' Partnership". However, so far, this institution has not yet begun to operate and only the future will show what will come of it. At Lebags, for example, the Enterprise Council elected by the employees–shareholders, in reality fulfils the functions of the absent trade union. The examples of Elmach and Matools show that if any group can possibly use such bodies for the articulation of their interests, it is mainly middle management.

Conclusions

It is clear from the preceding discussion that labour relations are still in a period of profound change, and that a new model (or models) are yet to be stabilized. It is possible to point, however, to a number of key themes which will continue to structure possibilities in the labour relations field. In this early phase of privatization there have been a number of hybrid forms of ownership change in which workers have retained some nominal rights to share ownership. Experience from the case study enterprises, and more widely, suggests that in the late 1990s we shall see the formation of real property relations, in which management will continue to buy up employees' shares in order to get a controlling block, and the role of outside shareholders will increase. As a result, it is possible to anticipate that the idea of collective property (in which the employees prevail over the other co-owners) will diminish and a concentration of ownership and accompanying labour polarization will develop. In addition to these processes we can expect the continuing restructuring of enterprises, in which large concerns are transformed into divisionalized or holding company forms with greater financial autonomy for the subdivisions. This will give middle managers higher status and will make their role in enterprise change and development a key one. Within processes of divisionalization we can expect labour relations issues increasingly to be decentralized to lower levels. The slump in production, which looks set to continue because of the drop in demand, will result in growing unemployment. Evidence from the case study enterprises suggests that this may lead not to increased conflict but rather to a renewed sense of the need to pull together in the face of "mutual trouble". The trade union position in all this is likely to remain contradictory; on the one hand there will be disappointment at the increasing failure to sustain collective property, but on the other they will support management as the strategy for survival.

There is little evidence to suggest that in the near future the trade unions will transform their role and become a main force in initiating either bipartite or tripartite bargaining relations. It is much more likely that management will become increasingly better organized, and able and willing to take the initiative in creating new labour relations models.

Notes

1. For a discussion of the economic changes prior to the regime's collapse see D. Filtzer 1991.
2. The Russian research team comprises: V. Gerchikov (leader), N. Barkhatova, E. Gorbunova, L. Truth (Institute of Economics and Industrial Engineering, Novosibirsk), M. Demedhko (Krasnoyarsk), E. Kalakutina, M. Koshman (Novosibirsk State University students).
3. Money collected by the state from direct sale privatization was to be used for social protection measures.
4. The decree of the Russian Federation President, "On the organizational measures for transforming state enterprises and voluntary unions of state enterprises into shareholding companies" (from 1.7.92).
5. "Open type" joint-stock companies refers to those where stock is available on the open market; "closed type" refers to the method whereby anyone can buy stock, but only through the enterprise; stock cannot be bought on the open market.
6. "Regulations of state enterprise commercialization with simultaneous transformation into the shareholding companies of opened type" (enclosure to the decree from 1 July 1992).
7. In Russia, endorsement from employees or their representatives is required for changes of ownership. The consent of the Council of the Labour Collective is necessary.
8. The Act of Russian Federation Government, "About revaluation of main assets in the Russian Federation" (from 14 August 1992).
9. *Financial Izvestia*, 1993, No. 36.
10. During January–June 1993, the US dollar's exchange rate declared by the Russian State Bank increased from 417 to 1050 roubles, decreased in August to 984, and increased again in December to 1214 roubles.
11. According to data from the Russian Government Centre of Market Conditions, the inflation rate in 1993 was even higher – 4.5–4.6 per cent per week, or about 22per cent per month.
12. Minimum Consumer Budget (per month) for a man of working age in 1992-3, 1,000 roubles. Calculated by the author based on the data of A. D. Kolobov (Institute of Economics, Novosibirsk) and on official inflation rate for 1993.
13. For a discussion of Sotsprof and other independent workers' organizations, see Clarke & Fairbrother 1993a.

CHAPTER 7

Models of labour relations: trends and prospects

John Thirkell, Richard Scase,
Sarah Vickerstaff

Chapter 1 outlined and compared the principal components of labour relations models in the different countries. The subsequent chapters were based on evidence derived from case studies of enterprises. In this chapter, the major aim is to draw upon the evidence of these to show the dynamics of action at enterprise level, especially the organizational processes and the relationship of these to the national economic and labour relations models. A further objective is to summarize the distinctive features of each of these national models. We then consider whether there are trends that justify claims of a shift towards western European patterns. Finally, there is a discussion of whether some concepts developed for the analysis of Western models of labour relations can be applied to those that are emerging in eastern Europe.

Enterprises and national labour relations models

The organizational processes at enterprise level are shaped by the interaction between internal and external pressures. The major external pressures on enterprises are the collapse of markets associated with the disintegration of the Council for Mutual Economic Assistance (CMEA) and of the Soviet Union. These were reinforced by processes of macrostabilization and shock therapy in Poland, Bulgaria and Russia. For many enterprises in these conditions the key issue for management and employees has been that of enterprise survival. Accompanying these is the general trend towards marketization through the deregulation of centralized state control over prices, customers and suppliers. Further forces having an impact upon the enterprises are those of actual or impending legislation on privatization; of legal changes in labour relations; and of tripartite decisions on wages. All these external pressures and events are closely related to political developments in the different countries, although the timing and sequence varies. Generally, processes within enterprises are related to the increasing autonomy of top management. Specifically, this may involve internal mobilization to promote the outcomes of internal restructuring and ownership change, and this has some consequences for labour relations.

At the enterprise level, the case studies show that organizational processes and labour relations are affected and shaped by three main factors: (1) the economic environment; (2) internal restructuring of the enterprise; and (3) ownership change. These create both opportunities and constraints for emerging managerial strategies. In particular, there may be opportunities for the development of managerial autonomy from state (ministerial) control over the main issues relating to the operational management of the enterprise. For example, choice of markets, prices and supplies. However, in relation to organizational restructuring and ownership change there may be opportunities for other institutions – especially the trade unions and employee councils – to act, and for groups of employees to mobilize to protect or promote their interests.

The appointment or replacement of enterprise directors in eastern Europe has generally been recognised as a key issue which can significantly shape the strategy of an enterprise and have a potential influence on its labour relations strategy. Under the socialist system such appointments had political importance, and consequently Communist Party organizations and the ministries played major roles in these decisions. During the 1980s there was a trend in all countries to reduce such external political influences by extending powers to employee councils and/or elections by the general assembly of the workforce. Following political changes in Hungary, in 1990 the government required the election of directors in the expectation (which was not fulfilled) that this would lead to the widespread rejection of directors appointed under the previous regime.

The enterprise cases show some examples of how the replacement of enterprise directors before the main political changes of 1989 had very significant consequences for the development of enterprise strategies. In one case – Hungair in Hungary – the new director encountered opposition from groups represented by the trade union within the company who considered that his strategy threatened their jobs, and this contributed to the loss of his position. In other cases, newly appointed directors were able to maintain and enhance their positions. However, the later replacement of directors in Bulgarian enterprises in 1992 as a result of political decisions led in two enterprises to the active involvement of the trade unions in the process as well as that of local political organizations. In general, but not always, changes in the post of director were associated with increases in the degree of enterprise autonomy.

The case studies illustrate the process of organizational restructuring in the large plants which have been characteristic of production industry in Russia and eastern Europe. This restructuring has been concerned especially with establishing more direct links between the market and parts of the enterprise concerned with production, so that organizations are able to respond more effectively. Divisionalization typically has meant some decentralization of managerial control and some increase in the power of middle management. This can involve reductions in headquarters staff and, in some cases, may lead to the creation of joint ventures of divisions with foreign firms. A significant effect of divisionalization on labour relations has been to enhance the separation of employees from the "core" of the enterprise, partly through changes in the power of middle management but also deriving from changes in the basis of remuneration. Thus, payment within divisions could be linked partly to divisional sales and not to enterprise results. In addition to internal restructuring, there are also some examples of functions being externalized. The general importance of restructuring in larger enterprises is that it has been seen as a means of increasing organizational efficiency, but its success is dependent on the ability of middle management to assume new managerial roles. It is important not to over stress the autonomy of divisional structures as budgetary control is often still centralized; restructuring may change the system of internal accountabilities rather then genuinely devolve financial control.

Typically, the prospect of ownership change is identified by top enterprise management as an opportunity to secure increased autonomy. However, in situations where foreign take-over is seen as a potential threat of closure in order to eliminate competition, management and the workforce are in coalition to delay ownership change. The Russian chapter concludes that in some cases middle management uses the context of impending ownership change to press top management for the internal decentralization that would enhance their power.

It may also be argued that labour relations can impact upon processes of ownership change. The cases of Hungair and Bos Air show how significant workforce mobilization can occur to protect itself against the effects of ownership change. The Polish enterprises illustrate some of the factors influencing the process of internal mobilization and its outcomes. Thus, the weak market position of Powcom inhibited the mobilization process. At Medex, awareness of the threat of unemployment in the district assisted top management in overcoming the possibility of workforce resistance to strategies for ownership change. On the other hand, the manager of Poltools failed to mobilize a sufficient coalition of managerial and employee interests to carry through the process of ownership change. This can be attributed to a deficiency of personal managerial skills.

Trade unions in the enterprise and collective bargaining

The only cases where trade unions have been derecognized are in the two Siberian plants. However, in Polish Medex and in Hungarian J. V. Protection the trade union has only a shell organization, almost like prototypes of small privatized organizations. The evidence of trade union mobilization in defence of group/sectional/occupational interests comes from Hungair and Bos Air. The negotiation of collective agreements, including wages, is clearest from the Czech and Slovak republics, from Bulgaria and from Ferrocor in Hungary. Although collective bargaining has legal legitimacy it is arguable that at the level of the enterprise this is more as a result of top-down articulation deriving from the tripartite national agreements rather than a process originating in the enterprises themselves.

All enterprises have structures of distribution – rewards and differentials – which, with forms of functional organization, constitute lines of internal division. The issue is how processes of greater managerial autonomy, restructuring and change in ownership alter traditional structures of rewards and lead to new lines of division. The chapters on Russia and the Czech and Slovak republics point to new separations of interest within enterprises as a result of the greater rewards accruing to senior managers. The case studies show that the most radical attempts to change labour relations through the reorganization of work occurred in those enterprises with foreign ownership.

Among the values associated with state socialism were those of the duty of citizens to work and of the state to provide employment. Mechanisms of central planning were designed to achieve both full employment and the even development of the economy, so that the planned geographical distribution of enterprises was related to the provision of employment at centres of population. At the level of enterprises, the operation of plan mechanisms made it rational for enterprises to maximize the numbers of the labour force as a protection against the uncertainties of supplies. But as Chapter 3, on the Czech and Slovak republics, explains, the salaries of management were also linked to the size of the workforce. The creation of unemployment was regarded as unacceptable politically. In the post-socialist economies many firms in Russia and eastern Europe – including several of our case study enterprises – have found themselves in difficult economic circumstances. One reason for this has been the disintegration of the COMECON organization, which provided major production outlets for eastern European enterprises, and of the Soviet Union itself, where the organization of a large part of production and distribution was planned for the Union as a whole. A second reason was the effects of the policies of shock therapy adopted in Poland, Russia and Bulgaria, which had drastic effects on the finances of many enterprises. The question is: how far in this context substantial reduction of the labour force of the kind following from the logic of capitalist production was pursued by enterprise managements? The evidence from the case studies is that it was only followed at the foreign-owned company in Hungary, where the operational criteria imposed by foreign management led to large reductions in the labour force, and in Medex, where the Polish managing director achieved substantial reductions in the process of ownership change. In Russia and Bulgaria, workers were put on short time or laid off but remained registered as employees. This could be a less costly strategy than making them redundant.

The issue of handling the reduction of employment in enterprises which are the main employers in communities is illustrated by Springs, Floorplast and Ferrocor. In the first two cases, the number of employees has been reduced by the divestment of activities and the transfer of functions to other bodies. Thereafter natural wastage would reduce workforces gradually. At Ferrocor, labour relations policy was based on the understanding that in the short and medium term there would not be drastic reductions in the labour force that would have dramatic effects on the community. Management hoped that organizational restructuring would facilitate a strategy of "leaping forward". In some cases it was anticipated that reductions in the labour force would follow full privatization. The general conclusion is that there is a range of approaches to labour force reduction contingent on various factors, but that managers generally have been reluctant to make drastic reductions.

Political and economic influences on national models of labour relations

The development of national models of labour relations is connected closely to and partially dependent upon political processes in the different countries and the economic strategies they have pursued. Thus conditions of stability or instability of governments influence the scope for economic strategies and these, in turn, are conditioned largely by the economic inheritance from the socialist past. The larger the inherited foreign debt, and the greater the dependence on international agencies which results from this, the weaker the possibility of gradual economic reform. Economic "shock therapy" becomes more likely.

The political change in Bulgaria at the end of 1989 was followed quickly by a wave of strikes and the threat of ethnic conflict. In these unstable political and economic conditions the trade unions occupied a pivotal place in political change and were the leading agency in securing the establishment of new labour relations structures and mechanisms including tripartism and collective agreements. The imposition of economic shock therapy in 1991 made the consent of the trade unions to secure "social peace" essential politically. However, political stability was not achieved in the five years 1989–94, which saw five different governments. The issues of economic policies and the labour relations models were a continuing source of political conflict and, as the Bulgarian chapter explains, privatization was postponed repeatedly. Dependence on the unstable political process meant that institutional development in labour relations was spasmodic rather than incremental.

In Czechoslovakia (the Czech and Slovak republics from 1991) the peaceful political transition has been accompanied by the incremental development of national labour relations models. The economic legacy has made the avoidance of "shock therapy" possible and this has coincided with the relative absence of industrial conflict, and in the Czech republic, of low levels of unemployment. Unemployment in Slovakia has been higher and political development less stable. In contrast to the rest of eastern Europe there was no significant fragmentation within the trade unions at national level in Czechoslovakia or subsequently in the successor republics. Tripartite institutions were established at an early stage, in response to trade union requests and the trade unions have participated at national level in the process of economic reform. In both republics there has been a substantial and incremental, but as yet uncompleted, process of ownership change.

In Hungary the process of incremental change and development in the institutions of labour relations (in parallel with the reform of economic structures and mechanisms) preceded political changes. As in the Czech and Slovak republics, the economic inheritance made possible the avoidance of "shock therapy", and industrial conflict was very limited, although the taxi drivers' strike in 1990 facilitated the confirmation of tripartism and its continuing and incremental development. As in Bulgaria, initially there was fragmentation at the national level between the reformed trade union centre and the new one but, as in Bulgaria, the balance of power in terms of membership and influence shifted towards the reformed centre. The process of ownership change has developed incrementally but remains partial. Despite the "social market" approach and the absence of overt industrial or political turbulence there is extensive evidence of increasing loss of popular support for the government, which was decisively defeated in the elections of May 1994.

In Poland the first non-socialist government of Balcerowicsz was the first in eastern Europe to adopt economic shock therapy as the essential mechanism for the rapid transition to a market economy. The early legislation on labour relations was premised on the assumption of the existence of a market economy with a high level of private ownership and relatively little remaining in the hands of the state (Hausner 1994). The process of shock therapy and macroeconomic stabilization proceeded without the substantial process of ownership change that had been envisaged. Industrial conflict had been a significant feature of the socialist period and it was replicated in key branches in the post-socialist era. At the same time, in the political arena the competition between the political parties led to the failure to establish stable governments. The number of employees technically classed as being in the private sector increased, while the membership of both Solidarity and OPZZ declined. As in Hungary, the general elections of 1993 resulted in the return of a left-wing government.

In Russia the diminution of ministry control over enterprises occurred at the end of the 1980s. The emergence of widespread industrial action in the mining industry challenged the economic basis of *perestroika* in 1990 (Clarke 1991). Since 1991 the political process in Russia has been one of conflict and turbulence. In 1991–2 Yeltsin and his government sought to synchronize economic shock therapy and a programme of mass privatization. It has been argued that the strategy of Yeltsin, Gaidar and their foreign advisers was to transfer the Polish model of shock therapy to Russia for both political and economic reasons (Steele 1994: 293–306). Labour relations in Russia were shaped by the weakening of the state's control over enterprises, and the weakness of trade union structures to articulate between national, branch and enterprise levels. Thus the dynamics of the Russian model have inhibited the development of labour relations institutions of the kind that have evolved in eastern Europe. The withering away of state operational control over enterprises (although the capacity to extract taxes survives), and the large-scale process of ownership change has led to the enhancement of enterprise autonomy and management power.

Trajectory of national models

The aspects of the labour relations systems discussed in Chapter 1 that is, independent trade unions; collective agreements and disputes procedures; and tripartism, together with the provisions of new Labour Codes in, for example, Hungary and Bulgaria, initially imply the development of national models with some similarities to those of Western countries. This question of the trajectory of the emerging eastern European models has stimulated academic discussion about possible outcomes. Thus, Slomp has discussed the preconditions for the development of the northern European model and suggested that the "strength of unionism may point to a development towards that model, but that the nature of politics in particular could well lead to the southern European model or to a new model of labour relations" (Slomp 1992: 30).

It is clear that there are external agencies encouraging some transference of Western approaches and the accompanying institutions and mechanisms. The ILO's philosophy of social partnership has been seen to be appropriate by most trade union centres. Its most significant institutional expression, that of national tripartism, has been endorsed generally by the IMF as a means of securing social peace, especially in the period of economic stabilization. Trade union centres have referred to the various ILO conventions as standards for legitimating their claims for legislation and protection, and have drawn on advice from the ETUC. The declared goals of the central and eastern European governments to achieve membership of the European Union have also legitimized the labour relations mechanisms to be found there. The role of multinational companies in joint ventures and take-overs also provide another clear channel of transference in which Western styles and mechanisms of labour relations are transported to eastern Europe and Russia.

However, it cannot be deduced from this that there will necessarily be a trajectory towards a Western model of labour relations. There are two main and related reasons for expressing caution over this. First, the "path dependent" character of transformation in these societies suggests that Latin America, Spain or Portugal may offer more appropriate parallels for changes than do the northern European countries. As Jowitt (1992) has argued, the political legacy of the eastern European countries is authoritarian, and not liberal democratic. We would not go so far as to say that the future is wholly determined by the past, but at the very least we must understand the nature of the historical legacy and its impact upon current evolution. Secondly, the comprehensiveness of the transformation objectives suggests that the national labour relations models in Russia and eastern Europe, which are highly contingent or dependent upon the economic and political outcomes in these countries, are unlikely to be stabilized quickly. As Przeworski argues, "Market oriented reforms are inevitably a protracted process – the period from stabilization, trade liberalization, and privatization to resumption of growth is long" (Przeworski 1993: 133), and, one might add, uncertain. Thus we expect the emergence of not just one model but of a number of models which combine new and old elements, and some degree of transference of Western institutions.

Throughout the social science literature on the transformation of eastern Europe and Russia a debate rages between those, like the authors of this volume, who argue that we can only understand current processes of change by reference to the specific legacy of the past, as opposed to those more inclined to see events as a radical disjuncture with history which makes possible a rapid and dramatic transition to a market based or capitalist system.[1] These intellectual concerns are mirrored by the different paths taken by eastern European governments in respect of gradualist reforms as compared to shock therapy tactics. Any attempt to explain or predict the likely path of labour relations models in these societies must address these two interrelated issues.

It is incumbent upon those of us who argue for a "path dependent" analysis to specify what we take the continuing legacy to be, and to analyze the impact of differing contemporary strategies on that heritage. It is only beginning to be possible to do this now that we have a sound base of empirical material to build on. We attempt a preliminary analysis along these lines in what follows.

In Chapter 1 we outlined the main features of the "Soviet model" of labour relations and the minor (apart from Poland) variations from country to country (see also Thirkell et al. 1994). As Slomp (1992) argued, we can characterize the different western European labour relations models in terms of particular combinations of the three parties to labour relations (that is the state, employers and trade unions) and the three levels of negotiation (the national, the sector or branch, and the enterprise). Using Slomp's (1992) framework we can try to outline the continuing legacy of the Soviet model.

It is generally assumed that in a market economy the role of the state in labour relations should be limited to providing certain laws and regulations within which the free parties in industry are able to negotiate. The classical pluralist interpretation would see the state as a neutral party, whereas the neo-corporatist literature has pointed to the many situations in which the state will more actively intervene to co-ordinate interests. In eastern Europe there has been a widespread belief that the overthrow of the communist regimes will and should result in "the withdrawal of politics" from the enterprise. In practice, as our case studies have indicated, with the exception of Russia, the role of the state in labour relations at all levels remains considerable and is likely to continue to do so. Not least because the state is still a key player in terms of the ownership structure of industry (Hardy & Rainnie 1994), and because it has taken on the enormous task of transforming society and the economy. Thus, in many countries the state has been engaged in trying to develop Labour Codes and labour legislation for a market economy which does not yet exist.

The second actor in Slomp's (1992) model – the employers – poses a

particular problem for post-communist regimes. Here we see a fractur-
ing of interests: new entrepreneurial capital, often running small businesses who adopt the kind of unitarist stance to labour relations issues
typical of small business owners in many countries; directors and managers of privatized state enterprises, many of whom have begun to develop employment strategies not unlike those found in large Western
organizations; and, finally, managers in enterprises still owned by the
state who may have changed their basic orientations to management very
little. As we have seen in our case studies, the degree to which managers
are able and willing to take advantage of enterprise autonomy from the
state varies considerably. The potential for well-organized employers'
federations in these conditions are weak, apart from the continuation of
old branch-based alliances more traditional of the Soviet period. These
older forms of "employer" organization, which can be characterized
confusingly as "corporatist" are more likely to be a barrier to the development of Western-style labour relations than a help. In Russia, the mili-
tary industrial complex of employers is a significant force in relation to
governments and has a party to represent its interest, although it does not
appear to be a party in tripartite negotiations. It has been argued that the
most organized political forces in Russia are the left and the industrialists
(Lohr 1993). Thus considerable caution should be expressed over the
speed with which a definable "employers' interest" can be articulated in
the emerging labour relations models. There is likely to be a growing
differentiation in the approach of employers in the private, small business sector and the joint-venture and foreign-owned parts of the
economy, and of managers in the state sector.

The third party in the industrial relations system – the trade unions –
with the exception of Russia, have been able either to reform or to develop independently, to play a new role in labour relations. In the relative absence of other developed organizations to represent political
interests, the trade unions have presented themselves as credible partners in a reformed industrial relations arena. However, as yet the main
focus of trade union activity has been firmly on the national political
stage, and attention to either branch- or enterprise-based organization
has been relatively weak. Trade unions are also proving relatively
unsuccessful in organizing the emerging private sector of small enterprises. It is thus clearly in the trade unions' interests in a period of
transformation to orientate their demands to the national political stage.

If we turn now to the three levels of labour relations activity we can see that the national level dominates, but in the private and privatized sectors of the economy enterprise level strategies are beginning to develop. However, the legacy of huge enterprises and an economic structure based around heavy industry and manufacture tends to focus attention on national questions of privatization and restructuring, and on regional questions of survival. There is a distrust of branch-level organization as a hangover from the previous planning system. A number of commentators argue that Solidarity's strategy of regional organization which allowed it to develop in the 1980s now presents a barrier to the development of sector- and enterprise-based labour relations (Hausner 1994).

As van Hoof has argued, the forms of participation and involvement characteristic of the communist period have disappeared: "a vacuum threatens to form at the base of the labour relations system." (van Hoof 1992: 105). Only in Hungary have the earlier forms of participation been replaced by workplace-based mechanisms: the Works Councils. In Bulgaria, trade unions have been wary of attempts by governments to introduce Works Councils as an alternative channel of representation at enterprise level. In Poland too, Solidarity has preferred to argue for collective bargaining as the sole channel for representation rather than accept other forms of employee participation. The relative weakness of collective bargaining arrangements at branch and enterprise levels are hardly surprising given the slow pace of ownership change and the continuing economic and political turbulence.

This brief discussion suggests that the legacies of both the "Soviet" model, and the particular reforms to it in each of the countries in the 1980s, can still be seen in the evolving models of labour relations. The state is heavily involved in the running of the economy, and both managers and workers may still expect the state to rescue ailing enterprises. The trade unions are cautious of participation mechanisms other than collective bargaining, as they are seen as relics of "self-management" experiments. This analysis begins to sketch some of what we understand by "path dependency". However, we need also to consider how these factors are affected by the specific strategies adopted by post-communist governments. Changes in governments and whether the orientation of their economic philosophy is neo-liberal or social market can have significant effects on the approaches to labour relations and the distribution of political power at specific moments. There has been a basic difference between those governments opting for "shock therapy" and hoping to engineer economic reform rapidly, for example Poland, Bulgaria, and Russia under Gaidar; and the more pragmatic and gradualist approaches adopted in Hungary and the Czech and Slovak cases. The implications of this for labour relations is illustrated by the following issues.

In all the countries studied there has tended to be unrealistic expectations about the possible speed of reform and the hoped-for economic benefits of a move towards a market economy. The approach to change has been relatively "*bolshevik*" in the sense of believing that a centrally administered strategy can transform the economy rapidly. This has been the case especially in Poland and Bulgaria, where shock therapies were adopted. Przeworski has characterized the style of these policies as "technocratic", in the sense that they have been legitimized as necessary, technical instruments applied by experts: "the first Polish democratic government launched a program of transition to a market economy with the hope that by moving ahead as resolutely as possible it could avoid submitting reforms to public discussion, to political conflicts, and to the uncertain interplay of representative institutions. The architects of reform persuaded that their blueprint was sound – no, more: the only one possible. They viewed all doubts as a lack of responsibility. They were determined to proceed at all costs despite all the political pressures upon them" (Przeworski 1993: 182–3).

However, it is also possible to see this approach as a continuation of a "*bolshevik*" approach which assumed that the economy may be managed in a wholesale way and that a ruling elite is "in possession of the real but secret truth about the polity, economy and world affairs" (Jowitt 1992: 211). Such an approach may serve to reinforce traditional expectations that the state will provide. In this situation labour relations issues are likely to take a back seat unless or until worker dissent forces them back on to the agenda. In Bulgaria, the UDF government of 1991–2 aimed to pursue a neo-liberal policy to disengage from tripartism and to separate the trade unions from bargaining at the level of the enterprise, but was unable to carry it off.

In contrast, the legal and institutional basis of the Hungarian model was developed between 1990 and 1994 with a conservative government operating with a social market and not a neo-liberal economic framework. Here, the government recognized that social policy measures were needed to underpin the economic strategy if public support was to be maintained. However, the defeat of this government in May 1994 by the socialist party shows that even the more gradualist approach stores up expectations that cannot be met. The election of the reformed old communist parties opens up the possibility of institutional developments in the form of social pacts as a basis for further economic reform. In the former Czechoslovakia, tripartism and social dialogue were instituted from above in advance of major economic reform. It is believed that the gradualism of Klaus is essentially pragmatic and that tripartism and the social market approach will be jettisoned when circumstances allow (Mansfeldova 1994).

This discussion suggests that labour relations models are fluid, with unstable boundaries and functions; governments of an avowedly neo-liberal persuasion are prepared to enter into tripartite negotiation to avoid confrontation and in order to try to maintain the pace of economic reform. Notwithstanding this lack of institutionalization is it possible to conceptualize developments broadly as pluralist or corporatist, as a number of writers have attempted?

The Western concept of neo-corporatism has been used in discussions on tripartism (van Hoof 1992; Héthy 1991). There are also references to the concept of pluralism (Kozek 1993; Morawski 1994). There is, of course, a general issue about the appropriateness of transferring such concepts from other societies and especially the kind of operational definitions given to the concepts. Western writers have differed in their conceptualization of pluralism in relation to labour relations. Thus, Crouch (1993: 56–57) disagrees with Dunlop's (Dunlop 1958) view that decentralization is a necessary feature of a pluralist industrial relations system, and argues that bargained corporatism at the level of the state can be characteristic of a pluralist system. For Clegg (1975) pluralism is related to the acceptance of interest and pressure groups as legitimate institutions in the political arena; in industrial relations this means trade unions and collective bargaining. From a slightly different perspective Fox (1974) contrasted the unitarist managerial approach to industrial relations with the pluralist one and argued that they were the product of different philosophies and ideologies which underlie institutions. In relation to the political and labour relations models of Russia and eastern Europe it is clear that, in contrast to the previous centralized and integrated models, there are now pluralities of political parties and the separation of trade unions from the state means that, at one level, it is appropriate to conceptualize the transition, descriptively, as one from a model which institutionally and ideologically was unitarist to one mainly of institutional pluralism. However, it is necessary to differentiate between institutional levels and types of organization. As Chapters 3 and 4, on the Czech and Slovak republics and Hungary make clear, in small firms, trade unions are not usually recognized and managerial authority is strong – that is to say, labour relations are both institutionally and philosophically/ideologically unitarist. In the larger enterprises there is institutional pluralism and, as national reports make clear, increasing separation of interests. Nevertheless, it is clear that in some enterprises philosophical or ideological unitarism may co-exist with institutional pluralism. None-the-less, there are fundamental differences between some Western conceptions of pluralism and what currently exists in Russia and eastern Europe. Thus, one school of Western writers, for example Dahl (1982), has emphasized the role of the state as a "neutral" arbiter between the competing claims of interest groups and their organizations as a feature of pluralism. Later writers in the pluralist tradition acknowledged the asymmetrical division of power resources but still saw pluralism, and the liberal democracy at its heart, as a guarantee against a monolithic state (Held 1983). In the conditions of transition and transformation such an institutional configuration cannot exist because, irrespective of formal ownership changes, states are fundamentally involved in the operation of the economy in ways that directly influence those enterprises that are not foreign-owned or small private businesses. Thus, many enterprises depend on credit for survival and this is largely determined, indirectly, by state policy. A corollary of this is that although independent trade unions now exist, the autonomy of organizations of employers engaged in bargaining with the state is limited. Thus, although descriptively (and ideologically) attractive, pluralism fails to acknowledge the importance of the state in eastern European transformation. The legacy of a relatively weak civil society in most of the countries also cautions against the applicability of pluralism and its association with liberal democracy. As Bruszt and Stark (1992) have argued, there has been no great upsurge of democracy in eastern Europe, with the possible exception of Poland; weak communist states fell to weak societies.

The continuing salience of the state is more clearly recognized in those accounts which conceptualize the national models as "neo-corporatist". This derives initially from the significance of national tripartite negotiations in all the countries considered here, with the exception of Russia. It is not clearly neo-corporatist in the sense of any of the prevailing western European models, because of the relative absence of concentrations of employers representing private capital – unless one is willing to talk of corporatism without capital. There also remains the issue of how far tripartism is institutionalized, that is the extent to which the parties to any accord can deliver what has been agreed in negotiations. In the literature on western Europe, neo-corporatism has been conceptualized generally as involving a system of interest intermediation and public policy formation in which there is a degree of co-responsibility for policy development and delivery between the state and functional interest groups, particularly those of capital and labour (for example, Schmitter 1979, 1982; Lehmbruch 1979, 1982; Panitch 1979).[2] Neo-corporatism or tripartism have emerged in eastern Europe as a response to the real or perceived threat of political and industrial instability (Thirkell, Scase, Vickerstaff 1994; Héthy 1994). In the context of weak political parties the trade unions, as the only organizations with a mass base, have played a crucial role in helping governments to build a consensus and establish some legitimacy for reform agenda. However, the instability of these arrangements and the weakness of employers' organizations suggests that the term 'bipartism' or 'concertation' rather than neo-corporatism is, at least at the time of writing, more suitable to characterize the models. None of the partners to agreements at this point has the organizational solidity to institutionalize such arrangements over the long term, with the possible exception of Hungary, where the Works Councils could provide a mechanism for the articulation of national accords at enterprise level. The credibility of the initial post-communist governments to deliver their part of any political exchange has clearly been repudiated in recent elections in Poland and Hungary. Socialist governments may be able to forge new alliances or pacts around reform agendas and will certainly be under pressure to do so.

With the recent ascent of "socialist" parties in Poland and Hungary, and the increasing talk of "Social Pacts", one can perhaps hypothesize that, with the exception of Russia, policy concertation will continue to characterize the relationship between governments and industry, with the attendant consequence that labour relations remain explicitly politicized. By "concertation" we mean the attempt by government and industry to manage conflicts and co-ordinate their interests in policy formulation rather than the alternative of each issue being contested as it arises (Lehmbruch, 1984; Schmitter, 1982).[3] The alternative to concertation – contestation or pressure – is still viewed with considerable alarm by governments, state managers, trade unions and citizens alike. In this situation we might expect labour relations at enterprise level to remain relatively underdeveloped outside the foreign-owned or joint-venture sector, in the sense that the actors' attention is not focused on establishing institutions of collective regulation at this level. The stability of state-led concertation is likely to come under constant threat as the state struggles to deliver its part of the political exchange, and trade unions seek to restrain the demands of their memberships. On the other hand, the spectre of an unregulated progression to some form of market economy may, as it did in Bulgaria, lead the trade unions to be the major force for establishing policy concertation.

Within this broad scenario there clearly are national differences. In the Russian case, the collapse of the state machine and the relative autonomy thus accruing to enterprises makes the concertation approach unworkable. The failure of independent trade unions to develop, combined with the weak state suggests a likely path of development in which employers and management consolidate their position vis-à-vis workers, and develop unitarist styles of enterprise labour relations. In Poland and Bulgaria, the relative strength of trade unions makes the concertation scenario likely to continue, if in a highly unstable form. In the Czech republic the relative success of economic reform may weaken the need for policy concertation, although there are many who believe that economic hardship is yet to come. Hungary, the only country to have instituted a system of workplace participation through the Works Councils, may combine national level concertation with the development of more institutionalized regulation of labour relations at enterprise level and thus more nearly approach the neo-corporatist paradigm.

Such uncertainties pose many exciting challenges for the academic observer. Clearly, there is a need for further research so that emerging similarities and differences between countries can be described rigorously. Hence there will be the continuing need for detailed case studies so that the interrelationship between national and enterprise-level processes may be documented. In this volume, we have tried to bring together a number of contributions which, based upon the case study methodology, have attempted to highlight the ways in which these are intertwined. To undertake detailed case studies is, in itself, a difficult task, but this is compounded when the studies are required for the purposes of broader comparative analysis. Nevertheless, it is only through such a methodology that it is possible to explore the delicate interplay of "enterprise" and "national" forces that in their varying combinations constitute the emerging similarities and differences in the labour relations systems of the national economies of central and eastern Europe.

Notes

1. For a discussion of this debate in the economic literature, see Claque 1992 and Murrell 1992a; for the parallel disputation in political theory, see Bruszt and Stark 1992.
2. For example, the definition given by Panitch stresses both policy concertation *and* interest mobilization: corporatism is understood as "a political structure within advanced capitalism which integrates organized socio-economic producer groups through a system of representation and co-operative mutual interaction at the leadership level and of mobilization and social control, at the mass level" (Panitch 1979: 123).
3. Schmitter (1982: 263) makes a distinction between policy formation by "pressure" or by "concertation". In the case of a pressure system, affected interests stay outside the policy process, whereas with a "concerted" process interests are incorporated within the policy process.

Bibliography

Bartlett, D. 1992. The political economy of privatization: property reform and democracy in Hungary. *East European Politics and Societies* **6**.

Bendix, R. 1956. *Work and authority in industry*. New York: John Wiley.

Brewster, C. 1992. Starting again: industrial relations in Czechoslovakia. *International Journal of Human Resource Management* **3**, 561–6.

Bruszt, L. & D. Stark 1992. Remaking the political field in Hungary: from the politics of confrontation to the politics of competition. In *Eastern Europe in Revolution*, I. Banac (ed.), 13–55. Ithaca, New York: Cornell University Press.

Burawoy, M. & M. Lukács 1992. *The radiant past*. Chicago: University of Chicago Press.

Chandler, A.D. 1962. *Strategy and Structure*. Cambridge, Mass.: MIT Press.

Claque, C. 1992. The journey to a market economy. In *The emergence of market economies in eastern Europe*, C. Claque & G. C. Rausser (eds). Oxford: Basil Blackwell.

Clarke, S. 1993a. The contradictions of "state socialism". In *What about the workers?*, Clarke, S. et al. (eds). London: Verso.

Clarke, S. 1993b. Privatisation and the development of capitalism in Russia. In *What about the workers?*, Clarke, S. et al. (eds), 218. London: Verso.

Clarke, S. & P. Fairbrother 1993a. Trade unions and the working class. In *What about the workers?*, Clarke, S. et al. (eds). London: Verso.

—1993b. Beyond the mines: the politics of the new workers' movement. In *What about the workers?*, Clarke, S. et al. (eds). London: Verso.

—1993c. Post-communism and the emergence of industrial relations in the workplace. Paper presented at ESRC East-West programme Seminar on the Enterprise in post communist societies, 26–27 November.

Clarke, S., P. Fairbrother, M. Burawoy, P. Krotov 1993. *What about the workers? Workers in the transition to capitalism in Russia*. London: Verso.

Clarke, S., P. Fairbrother, V. Borisov, P. Bizyukov 1994. The privatization of industrial enterprises in Russia: four case studies. *Europe-Asia Studies* **46**, 179–214.

Clegg, H. A. 1975. Pluralism in industrial relations. *British Journal of Industrial Relations* **13**, 309–16.

Crouch, C. 1992. The fate of articulated industrial relations systems: a stocktaking after the "neo-liberal" decade. In *The future of labour movements*, M. Regini (ed.), 170–1. London: Sage.

Crouch, C. 1993. *Industrial relations and European state traditions*. Oxford: Clarendon Press.

Crozier, M. & E. Friedberg 1977. *L'acteur et le système*. Paris: Editions du Seuil.

Csákó, M. 1992. Obstacles to the transformation of labour relations in Hungary. *Szociológiai Szemle* **4**.

Cziria, L. 1990. The Czechoslovak attempts on the way to self-management in state enterprises. Circulated during the OECD conference on labour market flexibility and work organisation. Paris: September 17–19.

—1992. Collective forms of work organization in Czechoslovakia economic practice. In *Labour relations in transition in eastern Europe*, G. Szell (ed.), Berlin/New York: de Grutyer.

Cziria, L. & M. Munkova 1991. Kolektivne pracovne vztany v podnikoch CSFR. mimeo.

Dahl, R. A. 1982. *Dilemmas of pluralist democracy: autonomy versus control*. New Haven, Connecticut: Yale University Press.

Deppe, R. 1992. The trade union perspective within the process of change in the former GDR and Hungary. *Mitteilungen 1*. Institut für Sozialforschung.

Dunlop, J. T. 1958. *Industrial relations systems*. New York: Rinehart and Winston.

Etzioni, A. 1961. *A comparative analysis of complex organizations: on power, involvement and their correlates*. New York: The Free Press.

Federowicz, M. 1992. *Trwanie i transformacja. Lad gospodarczy w Polsce (Persistence and transformation. The economic order in Poland)*. Warsaw: Ifis.

Filtzer, D. A. 1991. The contradictions of the marketless market: self-financing in the Soviet industrial enterprise, 1986–90. *Soviet Studies* **43**(6), 989–1009.

Financial Izvestia, 1993, N. 36.

Fox, A. 1974. *Beyond contract: work, power and trust relations*. London: Faber & Faber.

Gardawski, J. 1992. *Robotnicy 1991. Swiadomosc ekonomiczna w czasach przelomu (Workers 1991. Economic consciousness at times of transition)*. Warsaw: Ebert Foundation.

Gerchikov, V. 1994. Report on the Novosibirsk region. Paper to the workshop on Labour relations in development – focus on eastern Europe, Tilburg, March 23–5.

Gordon, L., E. Klopov, I. Shablinsky (eds.) 1993. *Na puti k socialnomu partnerstvu*. *Razvitie socialnotrudovykh otnosheniy v sovremennoy Rossii: ot odnostoronne-comandnogo upravleniya k treksstoronnemu sotrudnichestvu*.

Hardy, J. & L. Rainnie 1994. Transforming Poland. *Labour Focus on Eastern Europe* **47**, 42–57.

Hausner, J. 1994. The formation of a system of tripartite negotiation in Poland. Unpublished paper given to the Hungarian Industrial Relations Association/ Hungarian Institute of Labour Research/ILO Roundtable Conference: Tripartism in central and eastern Europe, Budapest, 26–27 May 1994.

Held, D. 1983. Introduction: central perspectives on the modern state. In *States and societies*, D. Held et al. (eds). Oxford: Martin Robertson.

Héthy, L. 1988. Plant level participation in Hungary. *Osterreichosche Zeitschift für Soziologie* **1**.

—1991. Towards social peace or explosion? Challenges for labour relations in central and eastern Europe. *Labour and Society* **6**.

—1992a. Hungary's changing labour relations system. In *Labour relations in transition in eastern Europe*, Gy. Széll (ed.). Berlin: De Gruyter.

—1992b. Political changes and the transformation of industrial relations in Hungary. At IIRA 9th World Congress. Proceedings No. 4, Sydney.

—1993. Tripartism: is it a chance or an illusion? *Társadalmi Szemle* **2**.

—1994. Tripartism in eastern Europe. In *New frontiers in European industrial relations*, R. Hyman & A. Ferner (eds). Oxford: Basil Blackwell.

Héthy, L. & I. V. Csuhaj 1990. *Labour relations in Hungary*. Budapest: Institute of Labour Research. 31–2.

Héthy, L. & C. Makó 1989. *Patterns of workers' behaviour and the business enterprise*. Budapest: Institute of Sociology and Institute of Labour Research.

van Hoof, J. J. 1992. Between corporatism and contestation. In *Westbound?*, J. J. van Hoof, A. Slomp & K. Verrips (eds). Amsterdam: SISWO.

Hughes, S. 1994. Monoliths and magicians: economic transition and industrial relations in Hungary. *Work, Employment and Society* **8**.

ILO-CEET, 1994. *The Bulgarian challenge: labour market reform and social policy*, Budapest: ILO-CEET.

Japan Institute of Labour. 1993. *Industrial relations in Hungary. Their development in the post-socialist society*. Tokyo: Japan Institute of Labour.

Jarosz, M. 1994. *Spolki pracownicze (Employee-owned companies)*. Warsaw: ISP PAN.

Jowitt, K. 1992. The Leninist legacy. In *Eastern Europe in Revolution*, I. Banac (ed.), 13–55. Ithaca, New York: Cornell University Press.

Kameniczky, I. 1992. *Co-operation among trade unions*. ILO Expert Group on IR Development in Hungary. (Unpublished manuscript.)

Kaucsek, Gy., J. Poór, F. Ternovsky. 1992. Kis es közepes méretü Magyar-országi vegyesvállalatok menedzselésénck, munkaügyi tevékenységének jellemzöi (Management and human resource practices of small and medium sized joint ventures in Hungary). *Ipargazdaság* 2–3, Budapest.

Kolankiewcz, G. 1993. *Between the macro and the micro – the missing middle: connecting state and society*. Mimeo.

Kornai, J. 1980. *Economics of shortage*. Amsterdam, North-Holland Publishing

Köves, A. 1992. *Central and east European economies in transition*. Boulder, Colorado: Westview Press.

Kozek, W. 1993. Industrial relations in privatised and private enterprises: corporatism or pluralism?. *Humanizacja Pracy*.

—1991. *Analysis of replicable research*. *"Transformacja instytucji pracy w warunkach realizacji programmeu dostowowawczego"* (*"The transformation of the institution of work in conditions of the realization of an adaptive programme"*). Synthesis attempt. Warsaw: East European Research Group.

—1992. Typowe zachowania zalog przedsiebiorstw panstwowych w poczatkowym okresie przemian spoleczno-ustrojowych w Polsce (Typical behaviour of state enterprise personnel in the initial period of the social-systemic transformation in Poland). *Przeglad Empirical Report*. (Unpublished manuscript.)

—1994. Industrial relations in privatised and private enterprise: corporatism or pluralism? *The Polish Sociological Review*. Warsaw: Polish Sociological Association.

Kozek, W., M. Federowicz, W. Morawski 1994. Industrial relations in Poland. Paper to the workshop on Labour relations in development – focus on eastern Europe. Tilburg, March 23–5.

Ladó. M. 1993. Workers' and employers' interests – as they are represented in the changing industrial relations in Hungary. Conference on Transforming past socialist societies. Cracow, October 21–3.

Lehmbruch, G. 1979. Concluding remarks: problems for future research on corporatist intermediation and policy-making. In *Trends towards corporatist intermediation*, P. C. Schmutter & G. Lehmbruch (eds). London: Sage.

—1982. Introduction: neo-corporatism in comparative perspective. In *Patterns of corporatist policy-making*, G. Lehmbruch & P. C. Schmutter (eds). London: Sage.

—1984. Concertation and the structure of corporatist networks. In *Order and conflict in contemporary capitalism*, J. H. Goldthorpe (ed.). Oxford: Clarendon Press.

Lohr, E. 1993. Arkadii Volsky's political base. *Europe Asia Studies* 5, 45.

Makó, C. 1992. *From state corporatism to divided unionism?* Vienna: Vienna Institute for Advanced Studies. (Unpublished manuscript.)

—1993. Enterprise councils in Hungary: tools of management or tools of workers. *Kosmos*. Pittsburg: University of Pittsburg Press.

Marer, P. 1992. Transformation of a centrally directed economy: ownership and privatisation in Hungary during 1990, in *Privatisation and entrepreneurship in post-socialist countries' economy, law and society*, B. Dallego et al. (eds). New York: St Martin's Press.

BIBLIOGRAPHY

Mansfeldova, Z. 1994. Tripartism in the Czech Republic. Paper given to the Hungarian Industrial Relations Association/Hungarian Institute of Labour Research/ILO Roundtable Conference: *Tripartism in central and eastern Europe*, Budapest, 26–27 May 1994.

Moerel, H. 1994. In search of central and eastern European labour relations. Paper to the workshop on Labour relations in development – focus on eastern Europe, Tilburg, March 23–2. WORC Paper 94. 03.014/1.

Morawski, W. 1992a. Instytucjonalizacja stosunkow przemyslowych w warunkach zmiany systemowej (The institutionalization of industrial relations in conditions of systemic change). Warsaw: *Polityka spoleczna*.

—1992b. Trade unions in Poland: dilemmas of dependence, independence and relative autonomy. (Unpublished paper.)

—1993. Beyond industrial democracy: the coming of corporatism. In *Transformation processes in eastern Europe: Western perspectives and political experience*, J. Hausner & G. Mosur (eds), Warsaw: Institute of Political Studies PAS.

—1994. Emerging patterns of corporatist industrial relations in Poland: contextual mechanisms. Paper given to the Hungarian Industrial Relations Association/Hungarian Institute of Labour Research/ILO Roundtable Conference: Tripartism in central and eastern Europe, Budapest, 26–27 May 1994.

Ministry of Labour (Budapest) 1993.Tájékozatató a keresetalakulás és o kollektív bérmegaállapodás jellemzöiröi (A survey of wages and collective agreements on the basis of data in the first half of 1992).

Murrell, P. 1992a. Evolution in economics and in the economic reform of the centrally planned economies. In *The emergence of market economies in eastern Europe*, C. Claque & G. C. Rausser (eds). Oxford: Basil Blackwell.

—1992b. Conservative political philosophy and the strategy of economic transition. *East European Politics and Societies* **6**.

Neumann, L. 1991. Privatisation, employees, unions. *Társadalmi Szemle* **10**, 43–4.

—1992. Privatisation and Employment. *Európa Fórum* **2**, 4.

—1993. *Labour relations – on enterprise, plant level.* (Manuscript.) (Abbreviated published version: Budapest: Munkaügyi Szemle.)

Neumann, L. et al. 1993. Labour management relations and human resource practices in foreign and multinational enterprises. The Hungarian experience. At *OECD meeting of experts*. Budapest: 14–15 June.

OECD 1993. *Economic surveys. Hungary 1993.* Paris: OECD.

Offe, C. 1991. Capitalism by democratic design? Democratic theory facing the triple transition in east central Europe. *Social Research* **58**(4), 865–92.

Orolin, Zs. 1992. Vegyes vállalatok munkaügyi kapcsolatai (Industrial relations in joint ventures). *Munkaügyi Szemle* **121**. Budapest.

Panitch, L. 1979. The development of corporatism in liberal democracies. In *Trends towards corporatist intermediation*, P. C. Schmutter & G. Lehmbruch (eds). London: Sage.

191

Pankow, W. 1993. *Work institutions in transformation. The case of Poland 1990-92.* Warsaw: Ebert Foundation.

Petkov, K. & J. E. M Thirkell 1991. *Labour relations in eastern Europe: organisational design and dynamics.* London: Routledge.

Przeworski, A. 1991. *Democracy and the market.* Cambridge: Cambridge University Press.

—1993. Economic reforms, public opinion, and political institutions: Poland in eastern European perspective. In *Economic reforms in new democracies*, L. C. B. Pereira, J. M. Maravall & A. Przeworski (eds). Cambridge: Cambridge University Press.

Schmitter, P. C. 1979. Still the century of corporatism. In *Trends towards corporatist intermediation*, P. C. Schmitter & G. Lehmbruch (eds). London: Sage.

—1982. Reflections on where the theory of neo-corporatism has gone and where the praxis of neo-corporatism may be hiding. In *Patterns of corporatist policymaking*, G. Lehmbruch & P.C. Schmitter (eds). London: Sage.

Slomp, H. 1992. Westbound, the northern or the southern trail? In *Westbound?*, J. J. van Hoof, A. Slomp & K. Verrips (eds). Amsterdam: SISWO.

Stark, D. 1990. Privatization in Hungary: from plan to market or from plan to clan. *East European Politics and Societies* **4**(3), 351-92.

—1992. Path dependence and privatization strategies in east central Europe. *East European Politics and Societies* **6**, 48-51.

Steele, J. 1994. *Eternal Russia.* London: Faber & Faber.

Tardos, M. 1992. Property relations in the period of transition. In *Privatization and entrepreneurship in post-socialist societies*, Dallego et al. (eds), New York: St Martin's Press.

Thirkell, J. E. M. & E. Tseneva 1992. Bulgarian labour relations in transition: tripartism and collective bargaining. *International Labour Review* **131**(3), 365.

Thirkell, J. E. M., B. Atanasov, G. Gradev 1994. Trade unions, political parties and governments in Bulgaria 1989-92. In *Parties, trade unions and society in east-central Europe*, M. Waller & M. Myant (eds). Ilford: Frank Cass.

Thirkell, J. E. M., R. Scase & S. Vickerstaff 1994. Labour relations in transition in eastern Europe. *Industrial Relations Journal* **2**(25), 84-95.

Thompson, P. & C. Smith 1992. Socialism and the labour process in theory and practice. In *Labour in transition*, P. Thompson & C. Smith (eds). London: Routledge.

Tyszkiewicz, M. 1992. Jacek Kuron's new economic policy. *Labour Focus on Eastern Europe* **43**, 31-3.

Wildavsky, A. & H. Pressman 1974. *Implementation.* New York: Basic Books.

Index